Tampa Cigar Workers

Florida A&M University, Tallahassee
Florida Atlantic University, Boca Raton
Florida Gulf Coast University, Ft. Myers
Florida International University, Miami
Florida State University, Tallahassee
University of Central Florida, Orlando
University of Florida, Gainesville
University of North Florida, Jacksonville
University of South Florida, Tampa
University of West Florida, Pensacola

University Press of Florida

Gainesville · Tallahassee · Tampa · Boca Raton

Pensacola · Orlando · Miami · Jacksonville · Ft. Myers

Tampa Cigar Workers

A Pictorial History

Robert P. Ingalls and Louis A. Pérez, Jr.

08 07 06 05 04 03   6 5 4 3 2 1

Library of Congress Cataloging-in-Publication Data
Ingalls, Robert P., 1941–
Tampa cigar workers: a pictorial history / Robert P. Ingalls
and Louis A. Pérez, Jr.
p. cm.
ISBN 0-8130-2602-4 (cloth: alk paper)
1. Cigar makers—Florida—Tampa—History. 2. Cuban Americans—
Employment—Florida—Tampa—History. 3. Cigar industry—
Florida—Tampa—History. I. Pérez, Louis A., 1943–. II. Title.
HD8039.C542 U65 2003
331.7′67972′0975965—dc21 2002028936

The University Press of Florida is the scholarly publishing agency
for the State University System of Florida, comprising Florida A&M
University, Florida Atlantic University, Florida Gulf Coast University,
Florida International University, Florida State University, University
of Central Florida, University of Florida, University of North Florida,
University of South Florida, and University of West Florida.

University Press of Florida
15 Northwest 15th Street
Gainesville, FL 32611–2079
http://www.upf.com

To the memory of
Tony Pizzo and Jose Yglesias,
whose dedication to the history of Tampa cigar workers
made this book possible.

Contents

Acknowledgments

A number of people generously assisted in the preparation of this book. The project began in the Special Collections Department of the University of South Florida Library, which houses a rich array of photographs, documents, and publications related to the history of Tampa's cigar industry and the institutions sustained by immigrant cigar workers. Access to all this material is facilitated by a knowledgeable and cooperative staff, including Paul Camp, Larry Heilos, Gayle Penner, Pat Thornberry, and Pat Tuttle. Except where otherwise credited, all photographs in this book are courtesy of USF's Special Collections.

Individuals who graciously answered our appeal for photographs include Juan José Baldrich, Maura Barrios, Dalia Corro, Judy Deese, John Favata, Jack Fernández, Willie García, Rose Giglio, Nonita Henson-Cuesta, Art Maynor, James Leone, Patrick Manteiga, Dolores Partie, Al Sánchez, Arsenio Sánchez, Elvira Stoeltzing, and Ana Varela-Lago. The process of duplicating all the photographs and other illustrations was immensely facilitated by Richard Bernardy and Maggie Doherty, two members of the USF Library staff whose assistance proved invaluable. Susan Fernández of the University Press of Florida helped advance this project in its initial stages through her encouragement and advice. Gary Mormino generously shared his knowledge and research notes. We are especially grateful to Nancy Hewitt and Gerald Poyo, who provided careful and informed readings of the manuscript and made helpful suggestions.

Finally, we dedicate this book to the memory of Tony Pizzo and Jose Yglesias, who long appreciated the significance of Tampa's immigrant community and who, each in his own way, documented the lives of cigar workers. We remember them fondly and hope this book reflects our enduring debt to them.

The World of Tampa Cigar Workers

The story of Tampa cigar workers begins in Cuba. In 1878, the Ten Years War (1868–78) came to an unheralded end in the interior of Camagüey Province in eastern Cuba. A decade after the "Grito de Yara" had summoned Cubans to a war of national liberation, Cubans and Spaniards met in the remote village of Zanjón to negotiate a formal, if only ceremonial, end to the ill-fated struggle for Cuban independence from Spanish rule. The Pact of Zanjón (1878) brought to a close one cycle of immigration and precipitated the onset of another, with far-reaching consequences.

The outbreak of hostilities in Cuba in 1868 had set into motion the first in a series of population dislocations. Separatists unable to participate in the armed struggle, together with thousands of family members seeking to escape the anticipated wrath of the Spanish colonial regime, scattered throughout Europe, Latin America, and the United States. By the end of the first year of armed struggle, an estimated 100,000 Cubans had sought refuge abroad.

A peculiar broadcast fixed the distribution of Cuban exiles. A small group of separatists, representatives largely of the creole planter class, capable of enjoying a felicitous exile, settled in Europe, principally in Paris. Other separatists, consisting in the main of middle-class professionals, merchants, and entrepreneurs of various types, emigrated to New York, Boston, Philadelphia, and New Orleans. A third group, and by far the largest, consisted of Cuban cigar workers. Unable to sustain exile without employment, these workers tended to settle in the southeastern portion of the United States, notably in Florida, first in Key West and later in Tampa, Ocala, and Jacksonville.

Political unrest in Cuba unfolded against a larger economic drama. By the middle of the nineteenth century, key sectors of the Cuban economy had become dependent on the North American market. Economic dislocation in the United States had direct and often immediate repercussions in Cuba. The panic of 1857 in the United States precipitated pressure for higher tariff duties on items manufactured abroad. During the Civil War, moreover, a succession of laws raised the average tariff rate to a high of 40 percent. The effect on Havana cigar exports to the United States was immediate: Panic gripped Cuban manufacturers, and many factories went into bankruptcy and ceased operations.

The disruption of the Havana factories resulted in a major reorganization of the industry. Several more resourceful manufacturers, seeking to penetrate the North American tariff wall, relocated their operations to the United States. Since the 1830s, Key West had served as a site of modest cigar manufacturing. By the 1860s, the town provided Cuban manufacturers an ideal setting for the production of the much-coveted Havana cigar. Key West offered easy access to the tobacco-growing regions of western Cuba and the commercial centers of Havana. No less important, the skilled labor required to produce cigars was readily available. In 1869, as the war in Cuba deepened, the Spanish cigar manufacturer Vicente Martínez Ybor left Havana and established his El Príncipe de Gales factory in Key West. From this modest beginning, Key West emerged within a decade as a leading cigar-manufacturing center in the United States.

Almost from its inception, the cigar industry in the United States was linked to developments in Cuba. Repression in Cuba during the Ten Years War contributed to swelling the émigré population. As wartime conditions in Cuba forced Havana cigar factories to close, many unemployed workers migrated to Key West in search of work.

At the same time, the end of the Ten Years War had far-reaching consequences for the Cuban community in Key West. After the Pact of Zanjón in 1878, hopes for Cuban independence in the foreseeable future waned among all but the most zealous patriots. The end of the war also freed exiles to turn their attention to causes other than independence. Nowhere did this express itself more dramatically than among the cigar workers in Key West. Patriotic ardor after 1878 yielded increasingly to labor militancy. Émigré cigar workers in Florida had a tradition of militant trade unionism that had propelled them into the vanguard of Cuban labor struggles.

The militancy of Cuban cigar makers was reflected in the central place occupied by the factory reader (*lector*). Hired by the workers themselves, the lector sat on a raised platform, perched above the cigar makers, and read from newspapers and novels, usually for two hours in the morning and for another two hours during the afternoon. Manufacturers sometimes complained about the radical nature of the texts read in their factories, overlooking the fact that the workers themselves selected much of the material, especially the novels, which were read serially after cigar makers voted for the book of their choice.

The class solidarity of Cuban cigar workers was expressed through a number of worker organizations. As early as 1865, Cuban cigar worker Saturnino Martínez founded the weekly newspaper *La Aurora*. In the following year, cigar workers in Havana province organized a number of associations, including the Workingmen's Mutual Aid Society of Havana, the Brotherhood of Santiago de Las Vegas, and the Workingmen's Society of San Antonio de Los Baños. In 1878, the workers founded the Workers' Guild and the Workmen's Center. In that same year, tobacco selectors founded the Society of Selectors. In 1892, cigar makers convened the first workers' convention in Havana.

The impact of these developments in Havana had immediate repercussions in Florida. The nearness of the island and the frequency of travel between Cuba and Florida, together with family and work ties, combined to make the world of the cigar workers on both sides of the Florida Straits a single universe. Over the course of the last third of the nineteenth century, many hundreds of thousands of Cubans moved constantly back and forth between the island and the mainland. They migrated to the United States to vacation, work, live, and plot revolution. Between the 1860s and 1890s, in the course of three wars, many tens of thousands of Cubans emigrated north, an exodus that assumed the proportions of a diaspora. By the early 1890s, an estimated 50,000 to 100,000 persons traveled annually between Cuba and the United States. Labor militancy in Cuba expanded into Florida. By the mid-1880s, strikes in the Key West industry had become commonplace. Beset by labor problems, several cigar manufacturers sought relief in flight and inaugurated a search for a new site for their factories. In 1885, Vicente Martínez Ybor settled on a forty-acre tract of land east of Tampa. Other manufacturers followed, and within a year the new factories of Martínez Ybor and Sánchez y Haya commenced production of handmade Havana cigars in Tampa. In 1889, a prolonged and violent strike in Key West caused a number of other manufacturers to move to Tampa. Another strike in 1894 led to the relocation of still more factories.

As Ybor City quickly mushroomed into a thriving, Spanish-speaking community, Tampa's native-born population watched with decidedly mixed feelings. Although clearly buoyed by the economic boom, city leaders also worried about maintaining social control over foreign workers who were pouring into Ybor City. Their concern led the city of Tampa to annex Ybor City in 1887, thereby extending Anglo political control over the infant community.

Tampa's other Latin quarter—West Tampa—remained independent until 1925, when it too was incorporated. Founded in 1892 by Hugh C. Macfarlane to compete with Ybor City, West Tampa was originally a 120-acre tract on the west side of the Hillsborough River, which separated it from Tampa and Ybor City. To attract cigar manufacturers, Macfarlane's investment company offered free land and even brick factories to employers who relocated to the new town, a move that worked largely to the disadvantage of Key West. The new manufacturers included A. Del Pino, Julius Ellinger, and Angel Cuesta. Their employees, numbering 3,500 by 1895, created another Latin enclave that resembled Ybor City. Indeed, as transportation improved and streetcars linked the two cigar centers, workers commonly went back and forth between the two communities for jobs, entertainment, and political activities.

Cubans and Spaniards in Tampa and West Tampa were soon joined by Italians, many of whom found jobs in the cigar factories. Originating in several Sicilian villages, the tide of Italian migration continued from the 1890s until the outbreak of World War I. Most Italians took up residence in the predominantly Spanish-speaking neighborhoods, where they earned a living as cigar workers and peddlers and learned to speak Spanish.

Tampa's expanding cigar industry attracted thousands of émigrés, who proceeded to create a world of their own. Around this population developed retail trade, service industries, and small manufacturing, all designed to meet the emerging needs of the new communities of Ybor City and West Tampa. Émigrés established medical and dental practices and all types of commercial activities, including small business enterprises, hotels, boardinghouses, and Spanish-language newspapers.

Cubans, Spaniards, and Italians opened countless numbers of retail stores, cafés and restaurants, pharmacies, barbershops, and *bodegas* (grocery stores). In Tampa the Valdés Brothers operated a successful dry goods establishment. Manuel Moreno de la Torre owned El Bazar Americano, which sold shoes, hats, and "Cuban-style clothing," and Manuel Viñas sold "Cuban- and American-style bread" at La María bakery. Marcos I. Sánchez operated a real estate office, Francisco Ysern ran the Salón Central liquor store, and Antonio Salazar managed El Central restaurant. Dionisia Estrada opened a dressmaking business, and Cirilo Pouble established the Academia Pouble, a private school for Cuban children. Miguel Montejo was proprietor of the Hotel Victoria, and the Hotel de La Habana passed through several owners before burning down in the early 1900s. "He who passes along Seventh Avenue or Fourteenth Street," Carlos Trelles wrote in 1897, "would not believe that he is in the United States, for such is the large number of Cubans that one meets and the many business establishments of all kinds that one sees in which all signs are only in Spanish."

Sicilian immigrants also found opportunity in the boom-town atmosphere. Pietro Pizzolato opened a livery stable and grocery store. After Gaetano Ferlita started a saloon in Ybor City, he branched out into the import-export business. His nephew Castrenze Ferlita first worked in local cigar factories and then opened a dairy. Stories of their success enticed other Sicilians to emigrate. Meanwhile, Cubans in Tampa won appointment to government positions and served as elected officials at all levels of municipal, state, and federal administration. Fernando Figueredo Socarrás served in the Florida Legislature and as mayor of West Tampa, as did Francisco Milián who was also a lector in local cigar factories. West Tampa's first city council included Vidal Cruz, Francisco Fleitas, Martín Herrera, J. D. Silva, and R. Someillán.

The émigré community encompassed a sufficiently large market to become the object of advertising campaigns by Anglo businessmen. In the mid-1890s, the *Tampa Tribune* introduced a new page, "Edición en Español," filled with Spanish-language advertisements from North American merchants and shopkeepers.

The relocation of Florida's cigar industry from Key West to Tampa occurred almost simultaneously with the resurgence of the struggle for independence. Largely inspired by José Martí, the exile separatist leadership worked tirelessly to prepare for a new war against the Spanish colonial regime in Cuba. Few responded to Martí's appeal with more enthusiasm than the cigar workers in Florida. Adding a powerful nationalist element to the radicalism of the cigar workers, Martí appealed directly to the communities of émigré workers in Tampa and Key West for support of a new war of national liberation.

The drive for independence in the 1880s and 1890s displayed several notable features distinguishing it from the effort mounted in 1868. The movement for *Cuba Libre* at the end of the nineteenth century received important material assistance and moral support from Cubans residing outside the island. Mobilized by Martí, émigré Cubans provided the initial leadership for independence. For Martí, Cuba Libre signified not only a nation free of Spanish rule but also one that would suppress racism, exploitation, and oppression. No other sector of the émigré community was more disposed by temperament and tradition to identify with Martí's version of Cuba Libre than the cigar workers of Tampa.

Martí made the first of a series of visits to Florida in early 1891. He discovered that he had not misplaced his confidence. By the end of the year, during a visit to Tampa, Martí announced the creation of the Cuban Revolutionary Party (PRC), dedicated to winning independence for Cuba. For the next six years, cigar workers in Tampa labored tirelessly for the cause of Cuban independence. By 1896, cigar workers had established forty-one patriotic clubs, thirty in Ybor City and eleven in West Tampa. These groups served as the vital backbone of the PRC. Throughout the 1890s they collected funds, promoted separatist solidarities, and propagandized in their communities. They also coordinated support of expeditions leaving Florida to fight in Cuba. Many cigar workers made individual contributions at the factory, donating typically one day's pay each week.

During the 1890s, men and women, blacks and whites, workers and manufacturers, forged a community of uncommon solidarity. The ongoing struggle for Cuban independence served to blur a host of social tensions as the community rallied to support liberation. Class conflict, racial antagonisms, and gender tensions were largely muted during the years of mobilization. Blacks and whites joined in support of Cuban independence. All through the late 1880s and 1890s, increasing numbers of women joined the wage labor force in the cigar factories. Data on employment patterns in the Florida cigar factories are incomplete but suggestive: Between 1887 and 1893 nearly 20 percent of labor force in the Tampa factories (1,100 out of 5,900) consisted of women.

The organization of cigar workers behind the independence movement halted all trade union activity. Indeed, for the duration of the war, class-based activities were considered incompatible with the nationalist cause and were all but formally banned by the separatist leadership. The PRC frowned on strikes, perceiving work stoppages as a threat to the independence cause. Class interests were subordinated to nationalism. In February 1896, a threatened strike in Tampa prompted Tomás Estrada Palma, the chief of the New York delegation, to visit Ybor City to urge workers to return to the factories on behalf of *Cuba Libre*.

The politics of class, moreover, became a secondary concern as both labor and management found themselves linked on the same side of the independence cause. Many leading cigar manufacturers, including Vicente Martínez Ybor, Domingo Villamil, and Cecilio Henríquez, publicly identified with Cuban independence. Eduardo Hidalgo Gato, the Key West cigar magnate and close personal friend of Martí, donated tens of thousands of dollars to the separatist cause. Benjamin Guerra, secretary-treasurer of the PRC, owned a cigar factory in West Tampa. At the same time, such noted socialist cigar workers as Carlos Baliño, later a founder of the Cuban Communist party, and Diego Vicente Tejera, organizer of the Cuban Socialist party, labored in exile as close collaborators of José Martí.

The end of the war in 1898 had an immediate impact on Cubans in Tampa. Peace transformed the meaning of exile. The émigré community, so long occupied with the cause of independence, faced an uncertain future. The era of self-imposed exile had come to an end. Yet the opportunity to return to Cuba opened painful choices. Many had come to look upon Tampa as home. It was the birthplace of their children and the place where they owned homes. News of employment difficulties in Cuba further cooled enthusiasm to return to the island. The war for independence had devastated the Cuban countryside and crippled the urban economy. Competition for jobs grew increasingly fierce as more than 50,000 soldiers left the ranks of the Liberation Army in search of work. In September 1899, the Havana Liga General de Trabajadores (General League of Workers) published a manifesto denouncing the lack of jobs for those who had labored faithfully abroad for the cause of independence. Thus, there seemed little opportunity now for those Cubans who had served the independence cause abroad to return and resume their lives on the island.

With the end of the war, social tensions surfaced in Tampa. Race relations in the Jim Crow South had to affect the émigré communities. Increasingly, white and black Cubans went their separate ways. "As Cubans entered Ybor City, they were sorted out," Emilio Grillo noted in his recent memoir *Black Cuban, Black American*. "With the exception of the local corner bar, which they could patronize, black Cubans did not share recreational activities with white Cubans."

The end of the war, moreover, had the immediate effect of lifting the moratorium on labor issues that had been deferred through the war years. For nearly four years, the cigar workers had labored under a patriotic injunction against strikes. As the patriotic moratorium on labor activity lapsed, increasing attention was given to working conditions.

The end of the war also affected cigar manufacturers. Peace in Cuba promised to restore and expand tobacco exports to the United States, but the age of the independent cigar manufacturer was drawing to a close. More than this, although it was not immediately apparent at the time, a way of life was coming to an end in Ybor City and West Tampa. The old-style cigar manufacturer, usually Spanish or Cuban, was about to be eclipsed by North American corporations. The tobacco conglomerates of the 1890s lost little time in acquiring extensive control of tobacco fields and factories in Cuba. By 1902, about 90 percent of the export trade in Havana cigars had passed into ownership by the North American tobacco trusts. At the same time, many cigar factories in Tampa were acquired by American corporations. In 1899, the Havana-American Company, a consortium of cigar factories in New York, Chicago, and New Orleans, established ownership over a number of Tampa factories, including the one started by Vicente Martínez Ybor, who had died three years earlier. In 1901, the Duke Tobacco Trust made its debut in Tampa, and the Havana-American Company came under control of the American Cigar Company.

The new corporate culture brought with it new attitudes toward cigar workers. Increasingly, the pace of work in the old cigar factory, somewhat relaxed if not always efficient, was subjected to a new drive for efficiency and labor rationalization. Nothing better illustrated the new economic order descending on the Tampa cigar industry than the weight strike (*huelga de la pesa*) in 1899, less than a year after the end of the war in Cuba. The new management of the Ybor factory instituted a weight system whereby each cigar worker received a fixed quantity of tobacco to produce a specific number of cigars. Workers protested that the assigned lot of tobacco was inadequate, and they demanded removal of the scales. The manufacturers' refusal precipitated a walkout that won support from cigar workers in other Tampa factories.

The 1899 strike raised issues of far-reaching significance. Most immediately, the strike represented the first major labor-management confrontation in almost a decade and served as a harbinger of the decades to come. The introduction of the weight system, moreover, underscored the transformation overtaking in the cigar industry. The scales represented an early effort to introduce efficiency and accountability onto the factory floor. Quite apart from the workers' claim that the assigned weight imposed an unreasonable quota system, the scales struck at the long-standing if unofficial practice whereby cigar workers were granted small quantities of tobacco for their own personal use. A traditional fringe benefit was now being threatened. "Because of the individual nature of his work, and his product," commented Cuban sociologist Fernando Ortiz, "the cigar maker always was entitled to his own 'smokes'—that is, a certain number of cigars he made for his personal use. This privilege came to acquire a tangible economic value. The cigar maker could sell his smokes to a passing customer, and the manufacturer came to regard this as a part of the worker's wages, paid in kind. The attempt to treat this privilege as a part of the worker's wages gave rise at times to acrimonious disputes and strikes."

In the end, the strike was successful. The manufacturers removed the scales, and a uniform level of wages won approval. In the course of negotiations, moreover, the workers secured authority to establish workers' committees in each factory.

The 1899 strike had a galvanizing effect among Tampa cigar workers. The success of collective action encouraged cigar workers to create a formal organization. Long the organizing target of Samuel Gompers and the Cigar Makers' International Union of the American Federation of Labor, Tampa's immigrant cigar workers chose instead to establish a union wholly of Cuban origins. The organization of La Sociedad de Torcedores y sus Cercanías, popularly known as La Resistencia, resulted in formal links with cigar workers' organizations in Cuba. The world of cigar workers on both sides of the Florida Straits, divided by the war for independence, was reunited in 1899. For the next three decades, cigar workers in Havana and Tampa came to depend on each other for moral support and material assistance. In a larger sense, the organization of La Resistencia reflected the decision of émigré cigar workers to remain in Tampa and defend their interests in their new homeland within the context of Cuban working-class traditions. In more ways than one, it also signaled the transformation of an exile center into an immigrant community.

La Resistencia soon developed into an active force among immigrant workers in Tampa. In another successful strike in 1900, it outmaneuvered the Cigar Makers' International Union (CMIU) for authority to organize the cigar workers. With its growing power, La Resistencia reached out to other immigrant workers in Tampa, including bakers, barbers, and laundry workers. Strikes also spread beyond the workplace. In one instance, the destruction of a local bridge connecting Ybor City and West Tampa forced workers to undertake hazardous boat crossings twice daily. In May 1901, La Resistencia threatened a strike to force the cigar manufacturers to pressure city officials to repair the bridge. "We cannot get what we want by asking for it ourselves," explained one worker, "so we strike and the manufacturers obtain it for us."

The most dramatic confrontation between labor and management occurred in 1901, when La Resistencia took steps to guarantee the closed shop for its members who dominated most of the city's factories. In a July ultimatum the union threatened a general strike unless the manufacturers dismissed a small number of cigar workers who had joined the competing CMIU. When manufacturers refused to comply, La Resistencia undertook its most ambitious effort by calling out some 5,000 cigar workers, virtually the entire cigar labor force. The 1901 general strike extended into the fall. Support for the Tampa strike came from Key West and Havana in the form of statements of moral support and funds for the relief of workers and their families.

The solidarity of Tampa cigar workers notwithstanding, the 1901 strike came to an unsuccessful and violent climax. Vigilante squads and local police inaugurated systematic harassment of union supporters. Arrested strikers were offered the choice between jail or returning to the factory. A local citizens' committee organized by businessmen kidnapped thirteen union leaders and forcefully deported them to Honduras. Working in collusion with cigar manufacturers, landlords denied strikers extension of credit and eventually evicted workers and their families. Union funds deposited in local banks were frozen.

La Resistencia failed to survive the four-month strike, which ended in defeat for cigar workers and dealt a body blow to the union. Taking advantage of the aftermath of the strike, organizers for the Cigar Makers' International Union made inroads, and the union ultimately absorbed large numbers of immigrant workers. In still one more fashion, immigrant cigar workers were integrated into another American institution, one more step in the Americanization and conversion of exiles to immigrants.

As long-cherished expectations of returning to Cuba after the war subsided, Cuban cigar workers increasingly reconciled themselves somewhat to permanence in Tampa, where they were the largest single immigrant group. By 1910, the city of about 50,000 people was home to 14,000 Cubans, 7,500 Spaniards, and 1,500 Italians. "The Cubans and Spaniards depend almost altogether on the cigar trade for employment," a government report noted in 1911. "The Italians have shown themselves able to survive in other callings, but the majority of them are also dependent upon the industry." Tampa's cigar industry encompassed 150 factories, representing an aggregate value of $17 million, employing a labor force of 10,000 workers, generating an average weekly wage of $200,000, and representing 75 percent of the city's total payroll.

As immigrant cigar workers put down roots in Ybor City and West Tampa, they created a variety of institutions to protect and promote their interests. In 1891, Spaniards established the Centro Español, in part to defend themselves against "Cuban hatred because of the Spanish government in Cuba." Eleven years later, a splinter group broke away to form the Centro Asturiano. In 1894, Sicilian immigrants created L'Unione Italiana (Italian Club) "to promote fraternity, charity and social intercourse among its members." Preoccupied by the independence struggle and undoubtedly still thinking of themselves as temporary residents in exile, Cubans waited until 1902 to organize the Círculo Cubano (Cuban Club), which then split apart along racial lines. After experimenting with several different organizations, Afro-Cubans created La Unión Martí-Maceo in 1904.

These mutual aid societies built a series of majestic clubhouses with theaters, ballrooms, cantinas, and libraries. Both the Centro Español and the Centro Asturiano also constructed hospitals, which provided medical care to members and others who paid a monthly fee for access to the services. The clubs became centers of immigrant life with a variety of activities, ranging from plays and operas to dances and lectures. They also sponsored sports teams that competed against each other in citywide leagues.

During the early decades of the twentieth century, Tampa workers embraced a variety of radical ideologies, including socialism, anarchism, and communism. These political sympathies, combined with their militant trade unionism, put cigar workers in an adversarial and often tense relationship with their employers, who enjoyed strong support from Tampa's business and political elite. Strikes, walkouts, lockouts, and violence characterized labor-management relations in the cigar industry through much of the first third of the twentieth century. Indeed, the strikes of 1910, 1920, and 1931 were dramatic expressions of cigar worker militancy.

The very uniqueness of the community, its cultural norms and its labor traditions, singled it out for extinction. Much of the continued militancy of cigar workers through the early decades of the twentieth century was attributed to the role of the lector and the reading material heard on the shop floor. As the popularity of radical newspapers and novels of social protest increased among cigar workers, management pointed to the *lectura* as the principal source of labor agitation. Between the early 1900s and the 1920s, the very fate of the institution of the *lector* remained contingent on the outcome of periodic confrontations between workers and manufacturers. In November 1931, after thousands of cigar workers joined a union affiliated with the Communist party, manufacturers suddenly announced their decision to abolish the lectura: "Heretofore the manufacturers have, through agreement with workers, permitted the reading of matters of general news value, educational or instructive, but the abuse of this privilege through the reading of anarchistic propaganda has caused the manufacturers to immediately withdraw the privilege of reading any matter whatsoever." Despite protests from cigar workers, manufacturers held firm, backed by government officials and local vigilante groups. As a result, the practice of reading disappeared from Tampa cigar factories in 1931.

The removal of readers did not, however, eliminate the political activism of cigar workers and their families. During the 1930s, they raised money to defend the Spanish Republic that came under siege from the Spanish military and troops from Nazi Germany and Fascist Italy. In 1948, many of Tampa's Latins supported the presidential candidacy of Henry Wallace, who ran in opposition to President Harry Truman's Cold War policies, and in 1955, Fidel Castro was received enthusiastically by Ybor City residents.

Nevertheless, the decade of the 1930s marked a turning point for Tampa's handmade cigar industry and the Latin communities sustained by cigar workers. Just as the growth of cigar manufacturing in Tampa had originally attracted Latin immigrants to Ybor City and West Tampa, so too the industry's economic decline brought the breakup of these communities. During the Great Depression of the 1930s, demand for luxury handmade cigars plummeted as smokers turned to inexpensive cigars and cigarettes. Hard-hit manufacturers looked increasingly to cigar-making machines to cut costs and reduce their workforces. Because one machine could replace from ten to twenty cigar makers, desperate workers fought valiantly against the spread of automation, but their rear-guard action did little more than slow the process, as Tampa factories went out of business, relocated, or automated. After the downturn of the 1930s, Tampa's production of cigars steadily increased through the 1950s, but the number of cigar workers declined as machines replaced them and flooded the market with cheap cigars. In 1929, 13,000 cigar workers produced over 500 million cigars in Tampa. This number dropped to less than 300 million in 1933, then rose to 700 million in 1955, when the local industry employed 5,500 people—only 2,500 of whom still practiced the old craft of making cigars by hand.

The final blow to Tampa's remaining hand workers came in the early 1960s. After Fidel Castro took power in Cuba, the United States imposed an embargo against the importation of all Cuban products, including the tobacco that had made Tampa's cigars famous. Gradually, manufacturers found other sources of supply in places like the Dominican Republic, where they also discovered a cheap labor supply that they trained to produce handmade cigars for the limited luxury market in the United States. Even the brief resurgence of cigar smoking in the 1990s did not revive the handmade industry in Tampa. By then, thousands of former cigar makers had passed away, retired, or found other work. Those who still rolled cigars were aging reminders of a lost past that could be observed locally at places like the Ybor City State Museum, where a lone cigar maker still practices his trade a few hours a week for tourists.

The decline of Tampa's luxury cigar industry spelled the doom of Ybor City as a Latin community. In the 1930s, economic necessity created a new migration from Ybor City to New York City, where Tampa Latins found work in service industries like the restaurant business. Some returned to Tampa after World War II but usually not to Ybor City. Locally, the war produced a mass movement from economically depressed Ybor City to West Tampa and other areas that offered returning veterans better housing. The GI Bill provided educational opportunities and home loans that made the aging houses of Ybor City less desirable. As Latin residents departed from the city's oldest Latin neighborhood, so too did many businesses that had catered to them. After 1945, suburban sprawl dispersed Latins to new housing developments, especially in an expanding West Tampa that soon stretched far beyond the old city limits.

Immigrant institutions also faced hard times as a result of postwar developments. A new generation of upwardly mobile Latins, who did not work in any single industry or live in any single area, became less dependent on the old social clubs of Ybor City and West Tampa. Membership declined dramatically, and the clubs struggled to sustain their buildings and costly services, especially medical care.

The death knell for Tampa's Latin quarter came in the 1960s with Urban Renewal. The dream of rescuing Ybor City with some kind of redevelopment dated back to 1949, when the federal government created the Urban Renewal program. Various schemes, including a walled "Spanish" city with "bloodless bullfights," briefly captured newspaper headlines and then disappeared. Permanent change took the form of Tampa's Urban Renewal Plan for Ybor City, which city officials hailed as "the most important thing that has happened to Tampa since the cigar industry moved here." The 1965 plan promised to "preserve and strengthen the distinctive qualities ... of Tampa's Latin heritage and present-day Latin community" through a program designed to "rehabilitate, clear and redevelop slum areas." However, within a few years, it became apparent that Urban Renewal meant only the destruction of old Latin neighborhoods. Bulldozers destroyed over 600 buildings, displacing over a thousand families and leaving only a wasteland of deserted, weed-covered lots. "Latin Tampa as it once was is no more," the *Tampa Tribune* observed in 1969. "Ybor City as Tampa once knew it is gone, probably forever." For several decades, the only major new construction was government buildings put up by Hillsborough Community College and the sheriff's department.

Much of West Tampa suffered a similar fate. Cigar factories closed, Latins moved out of the old part of West Tampa, and Urban Renewal leveled substandard houses. As in Ybor City, an interstate highway cut a broad swath through the heart of West Tampa, leaving the remains divided into two parts.

The majestic clubhouses still stood intact, except for that of La Unión Martí-Maceo which did not survive the bulldozers, but it took more than buildings to preserve a distinct Latin culture. "What made Ybor City in the past was not the architecture," Tony Pizzo pointed out. "It was the people." As people relocated and their children and grandchildren assimilated into mainstream American culture, membership in the ethnic societies declined to the point where some were threatened with extinction. Even those with the largest membership curtailed services and recreational activities. The hospitals of both the Centro Español and the Centro Asturiano closed. Theaters and ballrooms were generally silent except when some outside group rented the space. "There is not much left of my home town," Jose Yglesias lamented in 1977. "It is scattered and broken up, and its old *ambiente* seems to me almost entirely gone. I am bitterly sad about it."

The remains of Ybor City were deemed worthy of preservation. Beginning in the 1970s, buildings like the Centro Español were saved from the wrecking ball and put to new uses. Abandoned cigar factories were refurbished to provide space for shops, offices, warehouses, and small enterprises. The vibrant history of Tampa's Latins became a source of nostalgia, but the preservation and reconstruction of Ybor City's past raises problems. History lends itself innocently, often indiscriminately, to a variety of purposes. The absence of the cigar from the refurbished cigar factory found a striking counterpart in the absence of cigar workers from some reconstructions of Ybor City's past. It emerged as an article of faith that the immigrant cigar workers' experience was on the whole a felicitous one, despite evidence to the contrary in the form of social tensions, labor disputes, and political turmoil during the first third of the twentieth century. The passage of time apparently dulled memories among all but some surviving participants. A consensus view minimized, if it did not ignore altogether, the infelicitous encounters between immigrants and their host community. The cigar workers "liked the American way of life," a tourist tract assured visitors to a local cigar factory. Somehow the strikes of 1899, 1901, 1910, 1920, and 1931—to cite only the most important conflicts— were denied meaning if not overlooked entirely.

Like a Phoenix rising from the ashes, Ybor City has been reborn in recent years as a kind of theme park for tourists and revelers who flock to new bars, restaurants, shops, and movie theaters. This born-again Ybor City is cleansed, purged of all original sin associated with immigrant radicalism, labor militancy, and social protest.

Nevertheless, evidence remains of the vitality and turbulence that characterized Tampa's Latin communities. Memories of cigar workers and images of the world they created are preserved in oral histories, newspaper interviews, photographs, and the writings of natives who grew up in Ybor City or West Tampa. Using surviving sources, we seek to re-create in this book the *ambiente* of these communities from their birth in the 1880s to their demise in the decades after World War II. All the quotations in this book are verbatim, except in the spelling of words that have been standardized for the sake of consistency.

A cigar brand created to honor Vicente Martínez Ybor, one of the Spanish cigar manufacturers who founded Ybor City.

"The portrait which is the center piece . . . is an admirable likeness of the late Vicente Martínez Ybor, for many years a recognized leader in the clear Havana cigar industry of the United States, and the man to whose initiative is due the present proud position occupied by Tampa as a seat of that industry." (*Tobacco,* March 7, 1902)

"Florida's cigar industry began at Key West in 1831, when W. H. Hall chose the island city as a site for a factory, because of its climate and its proximity to Cuban tobacco fields. In 1868, with open revolution and business demoralization in Havana, many cigar makers migrated to Key West, where established factories offered employment. When fire swept the city in 1886, destroying the larger factories, and labor disputes further disrupted production, the majority of the manufacturers moved their plants to a district east of Tampa, which they named Ybor City for Vicente Martínez Ybor, one of their leaders." (Federal Writers' Project, 1939)

The Sánchez y Haya factory, the first to produce cigars in Ybor City, was located on the corner of Seventh Avenue and Fifteenth Street.

"Señor Vicente Martínez Ybor found forty acres of land he thought would be ideal for a cigar operation on his first visit to Tampa, in September 1885, and the small Tampa Bay town—population 2,376—was on its way to becoming a modern metropolis. By the end of the year, Ybor had purchased a total of seventy acres, begun construction of a cigar factory and fifty workmen's homes, and had allotted enough land for a factory site to Sánchez y Haya of Key West. Both plants were in operation by the spring of 1886 even though, ironically, labor troubles delayed Ybor's opening. Sánchez y Haya was the first to begin production. . . . The first clear Havana cigar was produced April 26, 1886, by Sánchez y Haya, and shortly thereafter, Ybor got his factory into operation." (*Tampa Tribune Florida Accent,* December 14, 1969)

"When the manufacturers and cigar makers arrived in Tampa, they found nothing but a stinking hole with swamps and pestilence everywhere. When we first arrived here, what little we found, in what was called Tampa, could not even be called a village. We made not only what Tampa is today, but the whole state of Florida. . . . We gave it life and placed it on the map of the United States. This state owes everything to us." (Enrique Pendas, 1936)

"It was the cigar industry, coming to this city in 1886, that was the incentive for a slow but steady growth of the little village of Tampa. . . . Its proximity to the tobacco fields of Cuba, and the always available supply of cigar makers in Havana and Key West are two reasons why Tampa has become a large clear Havana cigar manufacturing center." (*Tampa Daily Times*, December 24, 1924)

Franklin Street, Tampa's main thoroughfare, as it looked in 1886, when Ybor City was founded.

"The building is of brick, one hundred and sixty feet deep by fifty feet in width, three stories high, and meets every requirement of the largest cigar business in the United States. The first floor is divided into four general departments; the office is in the southeast corner, in the rear is the storeroom for boxes and the shipping department, and the packing department extends nearly the entire length of the building. On the floor above, four hundred cigar makers are employed, who, with the wrapper-strippers and selectors, more than fill the full area of space. On the third floor the tobacco is prepared for working by long experienced specialists in this branch of factory work. A large observatory on the roof affords a view of the surrounding country; the tract of land on which Ybor City is built, extending two miles east and about three-quarters of a mile wide, lies in the immediate foreground and Tampa proper can be seen still farther away in a southwesterly direction." (*Tobacco,* April 19, 1889)

The Martínez Ybor cigar factory, Ybor City's first brick building, as it looked in 1889.

Ybor City under construction in 1886. (Courtesy of Florida State Archives)

"We have rarely heard of a more liberal offer from capitalists than the one made this week by Martínez Ybor & Co., builders and proprietors of Ybor City, to their employees. A few months ago this company bought the tract of land on which the now thriving Ybor City is built, paying $9,000 in cash for the same. The land was then in the woods. They at once set men to work clearing the land, which was closely followed by the erection of neat cottage houses for the accommodation of their employees. Over 200 of the cottages have been built up to the present time. They are occupied by the cigar makers, who pay a monthly rent for them. . . . The company now proposes to sell these houses and lots to their cigar makers on weekly payments." (*Tobacco Leaf,* July 10, 1886)

"The people are greatly pleased with their new homes and have no desire to return to the 'old country.' They are orderly, well behaved, and industrious, but not very frugal." (*Orlando Sentinel,* quoted in *Tampa Tribune,* July 5, 1888)

"Mr. Martínez Ybor was offering homes for sale at a very low price. I, therefore, went to him and purchased a home at the corner of Eighteenth Street and Eighth Avenue for the price of $725. I still have this house, although considerably remodeled. I paid $100 cash, and the balance I paid off in monthly terms. I was able to do this with the help of my wife, who worked also at the cigar factory." (John [Giovanni] Cacciatore, 1936)

The Tampa Street Railroad connected Tampa and Ybor City from 1886 to 1893.

"The great curiosity to visitors is the Spanish-Cuban city of Ybor. A street railway runs out there. Trains drawn by a steam engine, with a first- and second-class car, run every half hour. It is a pleasant ride, and even if it were not, a visit to Ybor is worth some trouble. . . . Ybor is a miracle. Two years ago it was a wild wilderness; now there are hundreds of busy workers." (*Boston Transcript,* quoted in *Tampa Weekly Journal,* February 9, 1888)

A bird's-eye view of Tampa in 1892, showing the train (center) that linked the city's downtown (left) with Ybor City (center right).

Ybor City cigar workers at a soup kitchen during a strike in 1899 reflected the racial diversity and militancy that troubled Tampa's city fathers.

"The extension of our city limits [to incorporate Ybor City] is a matter of prime necessity to insure better law and order and the enforcement of proper sanitary regulations in our suburbs." (*Tampa Tribune*, April 22, 1887)

"Ybor City was taken into Tampa in 1887. . . . There were a number of minor disturbances and the Tampa authorities annexed the section to keep order there." (*Tampa Daily Times*, December 24, 1924)

"Ybor City is the Fourth Ward of Tampa, and there the residences are occupied entirely by the Cuban cigar makers and their families. These people have brought all of their customs and habits with them from the island of Cuba, and in visiting this part of the city, one comes in contact with an element as distinctly foreign as could well be imagined. Ybor City contains about 5,000 of these Cubans and plays an important part in the history and public affairs of Tampa. It is the city's financial soul, so to speak, as in this place the first cigar factory was built, thus inaugurating that era of wonderful prosperity which now characterizes Tampa, and making of her the second place in the world in the manufacture of clear Havana cigars, Havana only being first." (*Florida Times-Union*, quoted in *Tampa Morning Tribune*, June 23, 1895)

"I was born in the suburb of Los Sitios, Havana, Cuba, on September 21st, 1870. . . . On August of the year 1884, I was contracted as apprentice cigar maker at the factory of 'El Nuevo Mundo' of Ramírez and Villamil. I distinctly remember this place as I received many beatings, many blows, and very poor food. I had to remain there two whole years which seemed to me more like two ages. . . . Finally in the year 1890 . . . I came to Ybor City. However, I had to return to Havana in the following year due to the death of my mother. In the short space of one year that I had remained in Tampa I had foreseen that there was a wonderful future here, and accordingly I tried to induce my father to come to Tampa with my two brothers and sister. The first factory in which I worked was Lozano Pendas & Co." (José Ramón Sanfeliz, 1936)

"The tendency to leave cigar making for other occupations is very slight. The trade is one of the best paid in the United States, and offers such opportunities for the development of skill and consequent increase in earning power as to make it a desirable one in which to remain." (U.S. Immigration Commission, 1911)

José Ramón Sanfeliz in 1897.

Cigar makers in an Ybor City factory during the 1890s.

"Cigar-making as seen in Tampa, Ybor City and West Tampa is quite interesting. The people who do the work are Cubans, Spaniards, Negroes and Mulattoes. No women are employed as a rule [as cigar makers]. It is quite a sight to the novice to see the large second floor of a factory covered with benches, and men seated close together on either side of them, with a long pile of leaf tobacco in the center of the bench. All shades of color are seen in the faces of the men, from the pale of the full-blooded white Spaniard to the ebony of the Negro. Often the two extremes side by side, when the contrast is very great." (*United States Tobacco Journal*, July 25, 1896)

"To Cubans is owed the credit for the founding of the Fourth Ward of Tampa, that is Ybor City, where its residents produce wealth that is enjoyed by the very people who look upon Cubans with contempt. . . . This state of Florida, previously impoverished, is today one of the most prosperous states in the country, thanks to the development of Cuban cigars brought by the very people upon whom scorn is heaped." (*Cuba* [Tampa], September 9, 1893)

"Black Cuban cigar makers were an elite. They were highly skilled and they worked in a very intellectual environment. . . . Some among the black Cuban cigar makers became poets, writers, artists, and musicians." (Evelio Grillo, 2000)

"Cigar workers usually and generally wear good clothes and are prone to appear after working hours neatly and freshly dressed. To the Latin workmen, especially those of the younger state, the daily afternoon or evening change is a necessity, and the women workers also follow that practice with a fidelity that becomes a fixed habit. Evidences of this love of good clothes is found in Tampa's well stocked and modern shops." (*Tampa Daily Times,* December 20, 1922)

Black Cubans, including Juan Monteagudo (left), worked in Tampa's cigar industry.

An early photograph of a cigar factory in Tampa shows both men and women making cigars. (Courtesy of Arsenio Sánchez)

"A respectable fraction of the workmen in tobacco are women—dark-eyed, olive skinned and Castilian señoras and señoritas—who until four short years ago lived their tropic lives in the patios and plazas of Havana." (*New York Herald*, quoted in *Tampa Tribune*, February 14, 1890)

"The Spaniards continue to profit by the custom established in Cuba of employing them in the more desirable positions. . . . This was especially true of the cigar industry. Whether because of an inherent contempt of the native or for some other reason, it remains true that the manufacturers, who were Spaniards, chose the managers, a majority of the foremen, the selectors, and the pickers and packers from among their own group. In the factories owned by Spaniards in Tampa this rule is still adhered to almost absolutely. Even in other factories the managers are most often found to be Spaniards. . . . In Cuba, the Spaniards seem to have relegated the Cubans to such positions as they were pleased to consider inferior. That is why the cigar makers of the island were Cubans, and it helps to explain how after generations of employment in the same occupation the Cubans came to believe that skill in cigar-making is their peculiar possession. . . . [In Tampa] Cubans and Spaniards depend altogether on the cigar trade for employment. The Italians have shown themselves able to survive in other callings, but the majority of them are also dependent upon the cigar industry." (U.S. Immigration Commission, 1911)

Francisco Arango (second from left), *the manager of the Ybor factory in 1902, held regular Sunday meetings with his foremen "to plan the following week's work."*

"I was born in the town of Santo Stefano di Quisquina, Sicily, on May 12th, 1860. . . . In the year 1885 . . . I decided to come to New Orleans where many Italians were living at that time. . . . Several friends described Tampa to me with such glowing colors that I soon became enthused, and decided to come here and try my fortune in 1887. . . . I had expected to see a flourishing city, but expectations were too high, for what I saw before me almost brought me to tears. There was nothing; what one may truthfully say, nothing. . . . All of Ybor City was not worth one cent to me. . . . In all, I worked twenty-eight years in the cigar factories." (John [Giovanni] Cacciatore, 1936)

"The first Italian trailblazers to Ybor City were from Santo Stefano Quisquina, Province of Agrigento, Sicily, a hilltop village dating to the Middle Ages. Gradually they trickled into Ybor City where a familiar environment existed. The trickle became a torrent. . . . Within the Italian area [of Ybor City] there was a scattering of Spanish and Cuban families. . . . Some of the Italians moved into rental cottages while others made purchases from Mr. Ybor on the installment plan. The Italian quarter became known as 'La Pachata' after a Cuban rent collector." (Tony Pizzo, 1986)

Giovanni Cacciatore in 1935 at the age of seventy-five.

Cigar makers in the Ybor factory (c. 1900).

"The great majority of the Italians who were attracted to Ybor City came with the aspiration of becoming cigar makers. The earnings were excellent and the cigar industry offered them an opportunity to quickly elevate their economic status. At the beginning they were looked upon by the Cuban cigar makers as interlopers and a serious menace to their employment. The Spanish manufacturers were adverse to employing Italians for fear of alienating the Cuban cigar makers. . . . In time, with their charm and goodwill, the Italians began to break the inner sanctum of the cigar factories. They started in the stripping rooms, stripping the center stem from the tobacco leaf, and in time were given the opportunity of learning to roll cigars. The strict system of apprenticeship usually required a minimum period of two years to become a master cigar maker." (Tony Pizzo, 1986)

"The first cigar makers were the Cubans from Key West, and then the Cubans from Cuba. Then came the people from Spain and the Italians. . . . They only spoke Spanish in the factories. The poor Italians couldn't speak English and they couldn't speak Spanish. So they had to learn Spanish." (Pedro García, 1965)

West Tampa homes of cigar workers.

"A canny Scot, Hugh C. Macfarlane, founded the City of West Tampa in 1892, when his investment company platted a 200–acre tract west of the Hillsborough River as a cigar manufacturing rival to Ybor City. Macfarlane offered factory sites and three-story brick buildings to any cigar manufacturers who would agree to locate in the area, recouping his investment by renting or selling homes to the workers." (*Tampa Tribune Florida Accent,* December 14, 1969)

"Quite a number of Cuban families have moved from Ybor City to the West Tampa cigar town this week. The Del Pino cigar factory in that place is now working 116 cigar makers and 80 strippers." (*Tampa Morning Tribune,* September 28, 1892)

"Most of the inhabitants of West Tampa are cigar makers, and their family life, folk-lore, sociology and industrial conditions are virtually the same as those in Ybor City. Very little English is spoken except in the stores. Signs and announcements on the store-fronts are mostly in the Spanish language. On the streets and in the homes Spanish and Italian are the prevailing tongues. . . . In 1895 West Tampa was incorporated with a population of 2,815. . . . By 1925 its population had increased to 10,000 and it was then annexed to the City of Tampa by a vote of its citizens." (Federal Writers' Project, 1937)

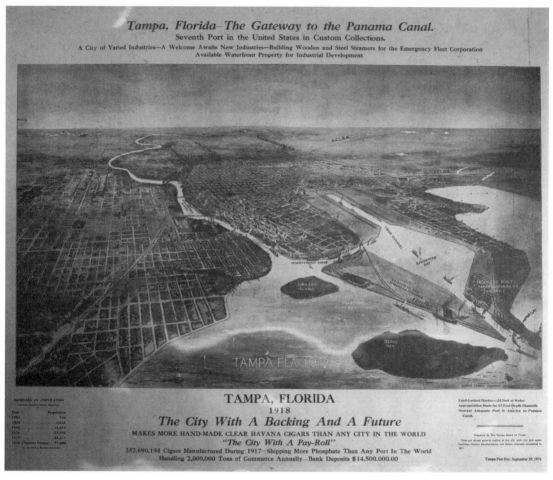

A 1912 map showing Tampa's downtown (center)—located between the Hillsborough River and the Ybor Channel—with West Tampa (upper left) and Ybor City (upper right).

"Céspedes Hall contains the best opera house south of Jacksonville. It is five stories high, with four towers and has two halls besides the opera house. The hall on the third floor is used as a lodge room for the different secret societies of West Tampa. The lower hall, divided into three rooms, is for the use of the members of the Sociedad Patriótica Céspedes de West Tampa, by which the building was erected." (*Florida Monthly: Tampa Number,* November–December 1895)

West Tampa (c. 1894). The tall building with towers was Céspedes Hall, a clubhouse built by Cubans and named in honor of Carlos Manuel de Céspedes, a leader of the Ten Years War.

Tampa's Franklin Street in 1905, just as a new state law mandated racial segregation on streetcars.

"Ybor City, with its millions invested in the cigar industry, has been and is still one of the chief factors in the wonderful growth and prosperity of Tampa. . . . Tampa is surely booming, and those who are watching her phenomenal growth will be more surprised than ever in the near future." (*Gainesville Record & Advocate*, quoted in *Tampa Tribune*, March 27, 1890)

"In the city, the question of handling the cigar makers comes up; and as you know, the Cubans comprise every shade of color, from the white man to the black man, and an attempt to separate the colored from the white people [on the streetcars] would necessarily result in trouble with the cigar makers; in fact it was stated to me that an attempt to separate the races in Tampa once before resulted in the separation of man and wife in some cases, and it had to be ultimately abandoned as a failure." (H. H. Hunt, 1904)

"The colored population are incensed at the operation of the Jim Crow [segregation] law that went into effect on July 1 and are boycotting the [Tampa] streetcars as much as possible." (*Tobacco Leaf*, July 19, 1905)

2 ⇒ The Struggle for Cuban Independence

Sombrero Blanco, a clothing store on Seventh Avenue owned by Romanian immigrant Isidor Kaunitz, was decorated with Cuban and U.S. flags on October 10, 1892, in celebration of Cuba's 1868 declaration of independence.

"The Cuban population of Ybor City and Tampa enjoyed a most eventful day Tuesday, October 10, in commemoration of the declaration of independence, which was made but never achieved. We trust, however, that this downtrodden people may yet throw off their yoke of bondage and attain that freedom and independence they so richly deserve. The residences and business houses were gaily decorated with flags, bunting, evergreens and sugar cane—representing one of the principal products of that famous island. The Cuban men, women and children were dressed in holiday attire and their faces beamed with all the enthusiasm peculiar to the natures of that sunny clime." (*Tampa Morning Tribune*, Weekly Edition, October 13, 1893)

"Since the early 1880s, José Martí had called on his compatriots [in the Cuban émigré community] to address the social divisions that plagued supporters of Cuban separation from Spain. . . . Tampa leaders were no doubt captivated by Martí's interest in a separatist ideal relevant to the expatriate working class, especially cigar workers. . . . Not surprisingly, then, Tampa leaders took the initiative to invite Martí to Florida in November 1891." (Gerald E. Poyo, 1985)

"As soon as Martí had breakfasted, he departed . . . to visit the factory of Ybor and Manrara. . . . Martí and his group went up the iron stairway that led to the entrance of the cigar factory. . . . Martí was introduced from the reader's stand. The cigar workers, rising from their stools, greeted the visitor with a noisy and prolonged banging of the blades of their tobacco leaf cutters [*chavetas*] on their work tables." (José Rivero Muñiz, 1958)

"Ybor City as a community was not quite six years old when Martí came here, but those cigar makers were not born yesterday. They were already well organized and they had not only their native intelligence and experience of life with which to judge a speech of Martí's; they had also the experience of listening to their readers in the factories for four hours of each working day." (Jose Yglesias, 1995)

José Martí (top center) on the steps of the Vicente Martínez Ybor factory during one of his visits with Tampa cigar workers.

"A party of the leaders and organizers of the Cuban revolutionaries in this country … arrived here from Key West on the *Mascotte* yesterday afternoon…. When they arrived in Ybor City they found assembled and awaiting them there nearly the entire Cuban population of the city. The crowd formed into a procession and marched to the Cuban lyceum, where a reception was held. . . . The secretary of El Liceo Cubano, who was master of ceremonies, proposed the toasts and responses were made by the following gentlemen: José Martí, Ramón Rubiera, Federico Sánchez, Ramón Rivero y Rivero . . . and two gray-haired señoras." (*Tampa Tribune*, July 18, 1892)

Ybor City's Liceo Cubano served as a meeting place for various Cuban organizations during the 1890s.

Tony Pizzo's handwritten description of the Liceo Cubano.

"I don't think I have told you about the grand emotions of my last day in Tampa, when in front of the Liceo which had flowed out into the street to hear us, a procession of Spaniards, hundreds of them, paraded in favor of Cuban independence. Extraordinary times are getting nearer. They paraded in the shade with their white banners. There were all sorts of dangers in the act, due to excessive trade unionism and allusions to local matters and anarchist slogans. A magnificent night! Thousands of souls; the occasion a most solemn one, of the few that can shake the human soul to its roots." (José Martí, 1892)

Paulina Pedroso, a leading supporter of Cuban independence.

"Certainly when Martí traveled to Ybor City, he did not lodge somewhere away from the community like a visiting politician, but lived right in its midst as he did with the émigré community in New York. . . . We have all heard that he stayed with the Pedrosos. . . . Only in the last couple of decades has it been emphasized that the Pedrosos were black. . . . To me, the significance of Martí's relationship with blacks such as the Pedrosos lies in Martí's opposition not only to slavery but to all prejudice that would keep him at any distance from friends such as they. He had first met them in Key West and then again in Ybor City, for they were active in the independence movement in both places. When in a 1893 visit to Tampa Martí was poisoned, Paulina and her husband insisted on taking him into their home. They kept boarders and they argued that he would be safer there. At night, Señor Pedroso guarded Martí by sleeping on the floor at the door to this room. I am not sure whether it was on this trip that having heard there was tension between Cuban blacks and some whites, he immediately upon his arrival gave Paulina his arm and insisted on their walking up and down the streets of Ybor City together to greet his friends. He was making sure everyone knew where he stood. He never compromised on matters of human equality—and specifically on the rights of Cuban blacks." (Jose Yglesias, 1995)

"For months knowing ones among the Cuban patriotic leaders in this city have said quietly to a few of the American friends: 'Look out, the war in Cuba is going to break out in a short time. Everything is ready for the signal.' Yesterday at 3 P.M. Fernando Figueredo received the following telegram from Gonzalo de Quesada, who was here recently: 'The revolution broke out on Sunday. The whole island is in arms. The *Herald* says Martí and Gómez have landed from Mexico.' The telegram was at once copied and sent to all the factories, and as soon as it was read the men went out in the streets shouting 'Viva la Cuba,' and discharging firearms in West Tampa. Many of them went to their homes to inform their families that the revolution had broken out, and men, women and children joined in the shout of liberty for Cuba. A meeting was at once called in West Tampa. . . . By seven o'clock a thousand people had gathered near O'Halloran's factory to hear patriotic speeches and show their feelings of joy at the prospect of freedom for their loved native land." (*Tampa Morning Tribune,* February 27, 1895)

El Mosquito *was one of several newspapers, including* Cuba *and* El Yara, *published by Cuban nationalists in Ybor City. This issue, dated March 9, appeared weeks after Cubans launched the war of independence in 1895.*

A page from the account book of José R. Sanfeliz, showing his collections from cigar makers on Saturday, September 14, 1895, for the Cuban cause. To the left of each cigar maker's name is his table number, and to the right the dollars and cents contributed, which totaled $22.10 for the week.

"In the year 1895 when the war broke out between Cuba and Spain . . . we organized the patriotic club of 'Vengadores de Maceo' (Avengers of Maceo). I was made president of the club, and was also in charge of collecting donations given by the cigar makers." (José Ramón Sanfeliz, 1936)

"In Tampa the poor cigar workers, with all their limitations but also with patriotic grandeur, work for Cuba. . . . I have said it many times: the revolution of 1868 was an undertaking of the rich, sustained by the fortunes of the men of the insurrection; this is the revolution of the people. The poor worked to provide the treasury of the revolution its initial funds." (Fermín Valdés-Domínguez, 1897)

"When we formed the 'Partido Revolucionario Cubano' (Cuban Revolutionary Party), a great number of patriotic clubs came into existence. . . . The outcome of the Revolutionary Party and the patriotic clubs was that twenty-seven expeditions were sent from Tampa against Spain [in Cuba]. At that time I was collector for the factory of Bustillo. I was in charge of collecting a certain percentage from weekly earnings of the cigar makers, in order to help finance these expeditions." (Domingo Ginesta, 1936)

"An immense mass meeting of Cubans and the friends of the Cuban cause was held at Céspedes Hall, West Tampa, Sunday evening. More than 2,000 people were present to take a part in the exercises. . . . The hall could not contain the eager anxious throng who were pressing to catch every sentence as it fell burning from lips set ablaze by impulses of Cuban patriotism." (*Tampa Morning Tribune*, June 11, 1895)

"The entertainment, given at Céspedes Hall last night in West Tampa under the Club Discípulas de Martí, ably assisted by the vivacious Miss M. F. Sánchez, was a glowing success. A large crowd of interested spectators enjoyed the festivities to the fullest extent and quite a sum was realized, a portion of which will go toward the Cuban cause, for which the entertainment was given." (*Tampa Morning Tribune*, March 18, 1896)

"This city contains by far the largest settlement of Cubans of any city in the United States, and more money has been sent from Tampa by the Cuban residents to assist in carrying on the warfare, than from any other city." (*Tampa Morning Tribune*, March 24, 1898)

Members of "Discípulas de Martí," one of the patriotic societies formed in Tampa.

Ybor City children posing with the Cuban flag in 1897.

"[At a rally in West Tampa] speeches were made by Fernando Figueredo, Ramón Rivero y Rivero, editor of *Cuba,* and others. Presently the name of Martín Herrera was called. It was stated he was in Key West on business, but Mr. Figueredo said his little ten-year-old daughter, Pennsylvania, is here, and she can make a speech. The child sprang to the platform, her large soft brown eyes fairly beaming with delight and her heart full of patriotic emotion for the beautiful island. The shouts of the large crowd of people were heard for blocks around, and then silence reigned. She began her speech, and for twenty minutes, she spoke *ex tempore,* in clear measured tones, giving emphasis to her well rounded sentences with graceful gestures which brought round after round of applause from the eager, anxious throng and not a few eyes were dimmed with tears at the pathos of her patriotic eloquence. It was a scene the writer had never seen before—a little girl pleading with the earnestness of a prince and the eloquence of a sage for the country she would lay down her pure sweet life to save from serfdom." (*Tampa Morning Tribune,* February 27, 1895)

"My Aunt Lila as a girl of four or five was given the honor of welcoming Martí by reciting a quatrain at the end of which she brought forward a homemade Cuban flag. . . . Those cigar makers of Ybor City and West Tampa were the significant makers of our history, not the Teddy Roosevelts and the Rough Riders." (Jose Yglesias, 1995)

"The open-air meeting held last evening in the courthouse square in honor of Cuba was liberally attended. Enthusiasm was at fever heat, and both the patriotic airs pealed forth by the Key West band and the stirring addresses delivered by the orators were liberally punctuated with applause. . . . But the speaking did not, as announced, take place from the band stand. When the excellent band mounted the platform, they were informed they could not use it—one official remarking that 'it was for white men, not niggers.' The band, therefore, took up its stand near the courthouse steps; and it was here, from a dry goods box placed behind a table with two kerosene lamps, that the speaking took place." (*Tampa Morning Tribune*, October 29, 1895)

"Tampa . . . served as the cradle of the glorious Cuban Revolutionary Party. The honest labor of the workers of Florida will remain always as a source of pride in the history of the *patria* [homeland]. The arms and ammunition—all—we owe in large measure to the honorable work, to the devotion and the sacrifice of the suffering cigar workers, those among the most humble, who will someday occupy an important place among the great men and women of the Cuban nation." (General Máximo Gómez, 1897)

Tampa's courthouse.

Cubans training in Tampa to join the fight against Spain.

"The enlistment of Cuban soldiers here [in Tampa] this week has made quite a stir in the cigar factories. About 300 unmarried men enlisted, and 600 to 700 more have arrived from Key West, Jacksonville, New York and other cities. They are encamped in West Tampa awaiting orders. Most of those who enlisted here are cigar makers, and their places in the factories are being filled rapidly by others, who are glad to step in." (*Tobacco Leaf,* May 11, 1898)

"If anyone were to doubt the patriotism, determination, and will of Tampa, if anyone were to believe that Cuban émigrés would accept anything less than the complete independence of Cuba, if those who speak of our brothers accepting compromises were to live and witness the enthusiasm, the unity of purpose, and the devotion to our cause that exists in this American town that is in its essence Cuban, that person would rapidly inform our enemy: cease and desist, your efforts are futile." (*Revista de Cuba Libre* [Tampa], January 8, 1898)

"Hostilities have ceased and the war has come to end. . . . Spain will relinquish all claims of sovereignty over Cuba. . . . The Cubans of Tampa are pleased at the end of the war." (*Tampa Morning Tribune,* August 14, 1898)

3 → *The Boom of the 1890s*

Ybor City's Seventh Avenue (at the corner of Fifteenth Street) in 1899.

"Ybor City, one of Tampa's flourishing suburbs, is at present experiencing a genuine boom in the strictest sense of the term. . . . While it is true that the progress and advancement of Ybor City is largely due to her cigar industries, it is equally true that she owes much of her present size and excellent business condition to the zealous efforts of her enterprising and progressive citizens. . . . As fast as business and residence houses are completed, they are immediately taken by tenants and it is difficult to supply the demand." (*Tampa Morning Tribune*, January 5, 1895)

"Cigar makers and leaf strippers were not the only newcomers [in Tampa]. Workers from Havana and Key West arrived with other skills, including tailors, carpenters, retail clerks and many others who, lacking specific skills, wanted to work at anything that was available." (José Rivero Muñiz, 1958)

"El Malecón is the name of a famous boulevard in Havana. . . . El Malecón also is the name of a toy shop on Seventh Avenue, a shop that has brought joy to thousands of childish hearts. It is owned by Francisco Carrera, who has given many years to making and importing toys, and was the first establishment of the kind opened in Tampa. . . . The Carreras came to the United States from Havana. . . . For several years he was employed as a cigar maker in a factory at Ybor City. One day he told his wife that he intended to resign and establish a business of his own. . . . His hands had long since tired of handling the brown leaves. . . . He would open a toy shop. It would be called 'El Malecón' to give it a home-like sound. And there would materialize things that brought happiness to children. . . . The toy shop . . . was a very small place—that first El Malecón—but it was sufficiently large for the toy maker, his wife and one child to move about and spacious enough for those first few toys." (*Tampa Daily Times*, November 20, 1925)

El Malecón, one of Ybor City's first stores, as it looked in the 1890s with owner Francisco Carrera standing in the doorway to the left.

The Ybor City office (1896) of Dr. P. J. Valdés, a physician who was a graduate of universities in Barcelona and Madrid.

"The forced emigration of thousands of Cubans from their homeland for political reasons brought to Tampa many prominent men from the island, among which were thirty physicians, ten pharmacists, eight dentists, six attorneys and many writers and poets, thus forming the basis of the intelligent and enterprising Cuban population possessed by Tampa." (*Tampa Morning Tribune*, May 23, 1909)

Ramón Sierra's dry goods store (1898), located on Seventh Avenue.

"The cigar makers of Tampa receive more than $5,000,000 each year in wages. . . . The greater part of this enormous amount is spent among the business houses of the city with a generous hand. The wage earners receive their money on Saturday of each week, and by Monday night following, the banks have received as redeposits at least three-quarters of this amount. Of a necessity this keeps trade lively, as can be readily seen by the prosperous merchants. . . . The store buildings thus far, with few exceptions, are unpretentious; in fact, many a profitable business is done in a frame structure so cheap and common that it might be termed a shanty." (*Florida Times- Union,* quoted in *Tampa Morning Tribune,* June 23, 1895)

"Walking about the city, under the glare of the electric lights, the visitor first notices the oddity of the signs to him, if he is an American and has not been much abroad. . . . One sign informs the hungry pedestrian in search of *pan,* that it is the only 'original' and genuine bakery of the place—where not only the bread but also the price is light; and, by the way, it is not amiss to say that the Cubans in Ybor make very fine bread, equal in all respects to the best French article of that kind and unexcelled by the Vienna product." (*Tampa Daily Journal,* March 5, 1890)

"Sidewalks in the early days were made of wooden boards, and the streets were of sand. . . . There were no street lights, and residents had to depend on kerosene lamps to guide them after dark." (*Tampa Daily Times,* November 29, 1940)

The bakery of Pardo and Brothers (1900), located on Eighth Avenue between Twenti-eth and Twenty-first streets, shows delivery wagons and drivers, along with homes of cigar workers to the left and stacks of wood paving blocks to the right.

"Las Novedades was born with the cigar industry. It was across the street from the old Sánchez y Haya cigar factory, the No. 1 factory in Tampa. In 1890, when Las Novedades was founded by its original proprietor, Manuel (Canuto) Menéndez, Ybor City was a tiny village, barely four years old. Ybor City's early settlers, primarily pioneer cigar makers, made Las Novedades their favorite rendezvous, and over Cuban coffee and Spanish pastry, called 'las novedades' or 'the novelties,' they would spend their leisure hours discussing the affairs of the day. Gradually the tiny coffee shop became known as Las Novedades, and in this casual manner the name of Tampa's oldest and finest restaurant was born. In November 1891, the original restaurant . . . was destroyed by fire, but reopened in 1892. . . . Later, Las Novedades began serving *arroz con pollo* [chicken and rice] and *potaje de garbanzos* [chick pea soup] to a few special patrons on Sunday afternoons. These dishes proved so popular, the small coffee shop soon became a thriving restaurant." (Tony Pizzo, 1972)

Las Novedades before the original building burned down in 1891.

The original Columbia Café that became today's Columbia Restaurant.

"The Columbia Restaurant was opened in 1903. It opened up as a saloon, a little café, and in time it became the gem of Spanish restaurants. They had a bar, which is still there; they served pastries, coffee, and short orders. It was a regular coffee shop, a bistro or a cantina." (Tony Pizzo, 1980)

"It is the rule for all cigar factories to start to work at 6 o'clock in the morning. At 9 A.M. they knock off for breakfast, starting to work again at 10 o'clock and working incessantly until 3 P.M. when the day of eight hours is finished. From 3 to 5 P.M. is the time the Cuban eats his dinner, the meal of the day. Most of the workers are single men, and they eat at restaurants, of which there are great numbers at Ybor City. The sides of these are of glass, which in summer are entirely removed, and the wide roofs extending out over the piazzas give a desirable shade. These people at leisure are jolly and jovial and seem to be incessantly chatting to one another. The unmarried men get together in fours, and are inseparable. An injury to one is the concern of all, and woe be to the man who inflicts an insult on one of them. They live together, eat, work and play cards together." (*United States Tobacco Journal*, July 25, 1896)

El Café del Palacio, located on the corner of Seventh Avenue and Fifteenth Street.

"The custom of living in public by means of open doors and windows, with cafés opening to the street, is followed here just the same as it would be in a Cuban town." (Nevin O. Winter, 1918)

"Latins are politically-minded. . . . They are as intensely interested in politics in their native lands as in affairs at home. Even the poorest has a favorite coffee house, restaurant, or private club in which to spend evenings in search of discussion and recreation." (Federal Writers' Project, 1941)

Angela Fernández with her brothers (c. 1905), who all worked as cigar makers in Tampa. The Fernández brothers were (left to right) Luis, Adolfo, Pablo, Jacinto, Juan and Carlos. (Courtesy of Jack Fernández)

"Collectively, the cigar makers dress very well. . . . It would be best for the tourist, or anyone else who wants to enjoy one of our local attractions, to go over and see Ybor by night—how the Cubans live . . . when off duty from making cigars." (*Tampa Daily Journal*, March 5, 1890)

Ybor City's Florida Brewing Company and Ice Works (1897).

"COME AND CELEBRATE: The Florida Brewing Company presents its compliments to the general public with a cordial invitation to be present at the formal opening of their new brewery on Monday, the fifteenth, beginning at 10 o'clock in the morning. Such hospitality . . . to drink, together with good music to whet the appetite, we shall take great pleasure in dispensing to you all, whether white or black, rich or poor." (Advertisement in *Tampa Daily Tribune*, February 13, 1897)

"The Florida Brewing Company, which celebrated its opening yesterday with a big barbecue and free beer . . . is a Florida enterprise that the people of this state should encourage by their patronage. It makes a superior class of beer. . . . The building is elegant and colossal; its machinery is of the latest and most modern make, while its capacity is adequate to any demand that can be possibly made upon it." (*Tampa Daily Tribune*, February 16, 1897)

"In the Labor Day parade in 1900, the Florida Brewing Company entered a float, a vast barrel from which Jim C. Mooney and able assistants disbursed real and excellent lager to thirsty Tampans on Franklin Street. One hundred barrels of beer were given away that day. Tradition says that by the time the parade was over there wasn't enough lager left in that barrel to intoxicate a mosquito." (*Tampa Daily Times*, March 31, 1927)

"The activity of the Italians in other lines of work is greater than that of the Cubans or Spaniards. . . . Italians support, without the aid of outside patronage, a number of wholesale and retail groceries, dairies, notion stores, dry goods stores, barber shops, bakeries, and saloons. The Italians also practically monopolize the street trades of Tampa. . . . One hundred and two licenses were issued in October of 1909 for the term of one year to Italian peddlers. . . . Fifty-six licenses were issued to fish, fruit, and vegetable peddlers, twenty-six to milk venders, eleven to ice venders, three to ice cream venders, three for the right to exhibit performing bears, and one each to a peanut vender, a scissors grinder, and an umbrella mender." (U.S. Immigration Commission, 1911)

The shoe repair shop of G. Marino Loto, at the corner of Seventh Avenue and Twelfth Street.

One of Ybor City's many fruit and vegetable stands that featured tropical specialties.

"The Italian fruit dealers, who seem to monopolize the local trade in green stuff, persist in keeping their tempting stands open throughout the night and in the small hours of the morning and often put in the time by roasting a supply of peanuts over a blaze of barrel staves for the next day's trade." (*Tampa Morning Tribune*, July 4, 1897)

"Many Sicilians went into business as soon as they learned about fifty words of English, enough to cope with the Anglo salesmen. Their clientele was mainly Cubans and Italians. If they opened a grocery store, a sign went up in Italo-English, *Grosseria-Italiana*. In some cases, the cycle was from pushcart to wagon-peddler, then to the privilege of a fruit stand and then a grocery store." (Tony Pizzo, 1986)

Mortellardo's "Grocery & Macaroni Factory—First in Ybor City."

The label for a Tampa cigar, showing that it was made from tobacco grown in Cuba.

"The best tobacco in the world comes from the Pinar del Río province of Cuba. The seeds are planted late in the summer, and when six inches high the seedlings are re-planted in the tobacco fields. When the wrapper leaves mature, they are cut and conveyed to field drying houses. Here they are hung to dry. When they dry, they turn from green to brown and lose their rankness. They are then taken to a warehouse, where they are classified, sorted and arranged for further curing, baling and storage. After being totally cured they are shipped to the factory." (*Tampa Daily Times,* March 22, 1924)

"The cigar is composed of two parts, the body and the outer covering. The body of the cigar is called the 'bunch.' The tobacco comprising the body of the cigar is known as 'filler.' The outer covering may be a single leaf called a 'wrapper.' . . . In the manufacture of cigars, tobacco imported from Cuba, known as Havana tobacco, may be used for both the wrapper and the filler. Cigars made entirely of Havana tobacco are known as 'Clear Havana' cigars. These command the highest prices in the market." (A. Stuart Campbell, 1939)

"Tampa still maintains its supremacy in the production of fine quality handmade clear Havana cigars. In the better factories the finest grade of Cuban tobacco is used. This is called *vuelto abajo*." (Federal Writers' Project, 1935)

"Few smokers of Tampa cigars, especially those made of Cuban tobacco, realize their cigars are the products of numerous skilled artists. In the various phases of manufacture, from the raising of the seed to the packing of the finished product, corps of experts preside over the destinies of the Havana cigar, as all 'smokes' made of Cuban tobacco are known." (*Tampa Daily Times*, December 24, 1924)

CLEAR HAVANA CIGARS

LEADING BRANDS

Queen of Havana Cigars

Long Established and Popular

CUBAN-AMERICAN MANUFACTURING CO., TAMPA, FLA.

Brands for Jobbing Trade and Progressive Retailers

A Big Seller

Mild and Fragrant

Made by

CUBAN-AMERICAN MANUFACTURING COMPANY

Tampa ~ ~ Florida

New York Offices: 78-80 Broad St.

Advertising for Tampa brands, emphasizing that they were "Clear Havana Cigars."

The S.S. Mascotte *leaving Havana.*

"[By 1888] old side-wheelers that plowed between Tampa and Key West were replaced by a newer and bigger ship, the S.S. *Mascotte.* This ship . . . extended its trips to the port of Havana in order to facilitate the transportation of incoming cargoes and passengers. It made the crossing between these two cities [Havana and Tampa] in less than twenty hours. . . . The S.S. *Mascotte* and the S.S. *Olivette,* both belonging to the Plant Steamship Company . . . made as many as three round trips per week, made necessary by the great number of cigar makers who unceasingly traveled in both directions and the enormous quantity of leaf tobacco that the Tampa manufacturers imported from Cuba for their factories." (José Rivero Muñiz, 1958)

"Procuring tobacco is the most difficult task of the clear Havana cigar manufacturers. All the local factories either have a member of the firm or one its most trusted members or employees in Cuba to attend to this most important part of the work. The tobacco is purchased in bales, and as there is no uniformity in the size of the leaves, the largest and finest being the ones used for cigar wrappers, it takes the greatest experience in selecting and pricing the stock. . . . After the manufacturer buys his tobacco, it is imported to this country." (Federal Writers' Project, 1937)

"The result of a century of experience has been to divide the typical cigar factory into five departments—the preparing, the stripping, the manufacturing, the packing and the shipping rooms." (*Tampa Tribune*, February 14, 1890)

"Workers in the 'casing room' loosen the leaves in the 'band' (a bunch of from thirty-five to seventy-five leaves, depending on the grade), and when they have finished with as much of the various grades and sizes as will be required for the following day's work, they dip it in rain water in order that it may be pliable for stripping the next day." (*Tampa Daily Times*, December 14, 1924)

Mojadores *moistening tobacco at the Perfecto García factory.*

*"Strippers" (despaldilladoras) at the Perfecto García factory in 1924, removing the
center stem from tobacco leaves.*

"When the imported Havana tobacco from Cuba arrives in Tampa, it remains in
sweating at the warehouses of the companies until it is needed at the factories. Then
the unstemmed filler is sent to the stripping department where it is stripped by hand.
The hand stripping operation in the Tampa plants is done almost entirely by women,
and is the lowest paid operation in the plant. . . . The wrapper tobacco is all stripped
in Tampa. . . . In this operation the entire center stem is removed, leaving the two
halves which are to be used as wrappers for cigars." (A. Stuart Campbell, 1939)

"Strippers" at the Perfecto-García factory.

"The manufacture of cigars [uses] two general grades of tobacco, known as 'wrapper' and 'fillers.' Wrappers are the best quality leaves as regards size, form, color, appearance, 'feel' and fragrance, and are used to roll or wrap around the body of the cigar, which body is made up of fillers or inferior leaves." (*New York Herald,* quoted in *Tampa Tribune,* February 14, 1890)

"After the stripping operation the filler is stored for curing. It is then blended in a special department, or mixed with tobacco from other plantations. This blending is for the purpose of giving different tastes or flavors to cigars. Each manufacturer has his individual formula for the blending of cigars." (A. Stuart Campbell, 1939)

"The 'filler men' loosen the packs and shake the tobacco little by little until each leaf is separated from the other. They then take so many bales or packs of filler from the Partido district of Havana province and so many from the Vuelta Abajo district of Pinar del Río province and mix it thoroughly together." (*Tampa Daily Times*, December 24, 1924)

"All of us cigar makers went to work dressed up like sheiks; a man wouldn't work in dungarees then." (Norerto Díaz, 1942)

Cigar workers (dependientes) *blending filler tobacco at the Cuesta-Rey factory. (Courtesy of Nonita Cuesta-Henson)*

Selectors (rezagadores) at the Sánchez y Haya factory.

"Stripped tobacco goes to the wrapper selectors. These men are highly trained in their work, having served at least three and a half years as apprentices. Two men sit at a barrel, on opposite sides, and each man selects from ten to twenty sizes of grade wrappers. They pay almost no attention to the actual color of the leaf, but judge their work entirely from size and shape of the leaf, the prominence of the side veins, texture ('oily' or 'dry' wrappers) and any discoloration which would disqualify an otherwise perfect leaf. In the manufacture of about eighty different sizes of cigars, approximately fifty different selections or 'grades' of wrapper are required. The wrapper selectors count the wrappers into pads of twenty-five leaves and hand them to the cigar makers, punching their tickets accordingly." (*Tampa Daily Times,* December 24, 1924)

"[My parents] were married in Spain, then they went to Cuba, and they had seven kids there. I was the eighth kid. I was born here. In 1906 the cigar industry was booming in Tampa. . . . They were asking for workers to move here. . . . My dad learned the trade in Cuba. He was what they call a selector. In those days it was all handmade cigars, and my dad had to pick out the leaves. They have these wrappers, they call them; they come in different sizes so naturally you're not going to give the big size, a real good leaf, to a guy that's making a cheroot or a small ten-cent cigar or five-cent cigar; so he would have to save that wrapper for the guy that was making the thirty- or forty-cent cigar. Cigar makers all had tickets, and they had to come to him. He would select the size and the color." (Al López, 1985)

Selectors at the Perfecto García factory.

A cigar maker (tabaquero) *in a Tampa factory with his gauge just above his* chaveta *(right) and cup of gum* (left). *(Courtesy of Florida State Archives)*

"When the cigar maker receives his pad of wrappers, twenty-five in a pad, he goes to the filler bins and gets his filler. He is then prepared to turn out the particular size he is working on. His only tools are a special board, about fifteen-by-eighteen inches, upon which to roll his cigars, a cigar maker's knife (*chaveta*), a gauge showing the length and thickness of the size he is working on, and a sanitary cup of gum tragacanth for sticking the 'head' of the cigar. The cigar maker first trims the wrapper by cutting very close to the outside edge of the leaf. He then forms the 'bunch' in his hand by placing the leaves one by one, judging the amount in his hand altogether by his long experience in the work. Each leaf is so placed that the tip of the leaf is always toward the 'burn' of the cigar and the side veins upward and toward the left. The cigar maker now has the 'bunch' finished and applies the wrapper by spreading it on his rolling board and stretches it properly as he rolls the bunch within. After the cigar maker finishes fifty cigars, he ties them in a bundle and puts his table number on a slip of paper on the bundle. These bundles are gathered up at night and taken below to the packing room." (*Tampa Daily Times*, December 24, 1924)

"A cigar maker is a *tabaquero*. . . . A cigar maker's knife is a *chaveta*. The Spanish for knife is *cuchillo, navaja*, etc., but a *chaveta* in Cuba is a particular kind of knife—a cigar maker's tool. The literal Spanish meaning of the word is forelock or key." (Federal Writers' Project, 1938)

Tampa cigar makers at the Perfecto García factory (1930).

"The average cigar maker takes from twelve to eighteen months to acquire his technique. Nearly all the cigar makers start as apprentices, first in the stripping department and later as helpers to cigar makers. In this capacity they supply the cigar makers with wrappers and other materials, and make themselves useful in many other ways. Sometimes they stay after working hours and help clean up the plant. . . . Some workers who are getting a small wage while in the apprentice stage, go to other factories and claim that they are experienced workers, and for a time get more money, it is said. They are soon found out. . . . The average cigar maker begins working in the factory at the age of sixteen." (*Tampa Daily Times*, March 22, 1924)

"At first the factories allowed us as many *fumas* (smokes) as we wanted, but then they put a limit of five (free) smokes for every man per day, then they cut it down to three, and finally they would give us none at all. So we used to sit on the tobacco to press it, then hide it in our underclothes and take it home to make our smokes." (Norerto Díaz, 1942)

"The pickers and packers are trained in their work of picking colors, etc., having gone through a course of nearly four years' training. They work in pairs—one picker (*escogedor*) and one packer to the team. . . . As there are more than 150 different colors in Havana tobacco, it is the picker's task to distinguish these and place them in piles accordingly—each pile representing a shade of color. . . . When he gets fifty cigars of one shade, and as nearly perfect as he can pick, he passes the pile to his partner—the packer—who from the fifty cigars of one shade again makes a selection by picking the four rows for the box. He puts the cigars in different part of the rows, trying to make a perfect 'blend' of the particular shade of color he is working on, thus 'shading' them from one end of the box to the other so that each cigar appears like the other to the eye. . . . In the banding department, girls take each cigar from the box, band it and replace it in identically the same position as when it left the hands of the packer. The box then goes to a table, presided over by a member of the firm, where each box is personally examined." (*Tampa Daily Times*, December 24, 1924)

Picking, packing, and banding at the Morgan Cigar Company in West Tampa (c. 1922). Standing (left to right): Thomas Morgan, Sr. (factory owner), Ramón Vásquez, and Bernardo P. Sánchez, Sr. (factory foreman). Seated were banders (anilladoras) Teresa González (left) and Belarmina Peláez. (Courtesy of Arsenio Sánchez)

A label for a Tampa-made cigar, emphasizing its quality and connection to Cuba.

"Tampa-made Havana cigars did not need advertising. They were known throughout the country by smokers of fine cigars. They were constantly in demand, and every dealer stocked them. Tampa manufacturers simply filled the orders with quality cigars as they came in." (A. Stuart Campbell, 1939)

"Tampa is recognized as the leading clear Havana cigar market of the world. The cigar factories, located in Tampa and West Tampa, number over two hundred, many of which employ over 500 workers. The estimated output of cigars during 1915 is placed at nearly 1,000,000 per day, employment being given to over 10,000 Spanish and Cuban workmen. The weekly payroll of these employees averages $250,000. In addition, three cigar box factories, two of which are the largest in the United States, give employment to several hundred men and women." (*Rinaldi's Guide Book to the City of Tampa, 1915–16 Edition*, 1915)

A float in a 1914 parade, featuring men and women making cigars at benches, bragged that "West Tampa Makes the Best Cigars, Employs the Best Cigar Makers and Uses the Best Cuban Tobacco."

*Carlos Manrique, a sample maker, with his wife, Isabel, and their children
(left to right) Violeta, Charles, and Wilfredo (c. 1900). (Courtesy of Art Maynor)*

"My grandfather, Carlos, was a sample maker for both Ybor and Sánchez y Haya in Ybor City. The sample maker made cigars that were new and being considered for marketing. Carlos's career was short-lived, and as my mother told me, he became ill in his early thirties. She remembered, as a small child, he had a rag or handkerchief covering his face from his eyes down until the day he died." (Art Maynor, 1997)

"No worker ever refers to a factory by the trade name or the name of the owner. Some of the nicknames are *El Paraíso* (paradise), not named for the ideal working conditions, but because of a type of tree that grew outside the door; *La Pila* (the spigot) because there was a water faucet next to the factory where people went to refresh themselves; *La Trocha* (the outpost) because the factory was out in the wilds of Ybor City at the time it was built; *El Naranjal* (the orange grove) because there was an orange grove next to the factory; and *El Reloj* (the clock) because there was a clock on its steeple." (*Tampa Morning Tribune,* November 25, 1956)

"Cigar makers usually have a keen sense of humor and are quick to give nicknames, some of which are quite clever. For instance, one end of the spacious room in which they work at a certain factory in Tampa was not as well heated as the other. To the cooler end they gave the name of 'Manchuria,' and every cigar maker in town soon knew where 'Manchuria' was." (Federal Writers' Project, 1938)

The Regensburg factory in Ybor City was known as "El Reloj" (the clock).

"Although women have been given little opportunity to learn the cigar-making trade in former years, they recently have been given the same privilege as men, and now many of these workers have become as skillful as the men. In some factories the percentage of the women workers averages from 5 to 30 percent, while in others more than 50 and sometimes 75 percent of the workers are women. . . . When they do take up the hand method, it is said that they make as good a cigar as the men, and sometimes better. They are said to be steadier workers." (*Tampa Daily Times*, March 22, 1924)

"My mother was a cigar maker, hand roller. She could make a cigar from start to finish. And what cigars they were. She would leave our house before daylight and return when it was almost dark. She would ride the streetcar for five cents, but most of the time she would walk twenty blocks or more to the factory." (Emilia González Alonso, 1997)

Tampa cigar makers during the 1920s.

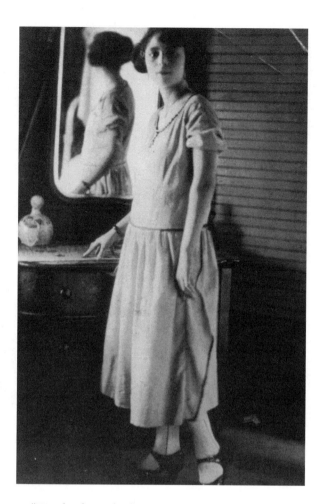

Dolores Río in 1923 at the age of fourteen when she started working in a cigar factory.

"Way back, at the beginning, it was only men [in the cigar factories]. . . . The only thing the woman could do in the factory was to strip the tobacco leaves. Italian women were strippers too. Italian, Cuban, Spanish, they all try to get on as rollers because they all want to make more money. . . . I went to the factory, Sánchez y Haya. I was fourteen years old when I started there. . . . I went over there to learn to make cigars, and I was working with someone teaching me, helping me. . . . My father worked there and my aunt." (Dolores Río, 1985)

"My first salary, you know how much it was? For that week, $3.25. . . . People say, 'Give me the good old days.' I don't want those good old days. Forget it." (Dolores Río, 1987)

"I worked until six, seven months before I had [my third child] Sylvia. And then I left because they fired me. . . . With [my first child] Gloria, I worked until the last day because then I was working in a little factory. . . . When my daughter Gloria was born . . . it was forty days when I go back to work. They call me. I say I cannot lose the chance. I got to work. I need money. . . . My mother, she took care of children of women who worked in the factories, three or four at a time. And when I marry and have children, my mother takes care of them too." (Dolores Río, 1985)

Young Tampa cigar workers in 1910. (Photo by Lewis Hine courtesy of the Library of Congress.)

"In many cases entire families of Latins have worked together for years in the cigar factories. Father, mother, sons and daughters worked side by side. Boys and girls of thirteen and fourteen were employed as apprentices. In some instances members of three generations are employed together. In prosperous times, with all members of the family employed except the younger children, the combined income of the family would frequently exceed $100 a week." (Federal Writers' Project, 1937)

"This is truly a city of the cigar, a symphony in smoke. Even the little boys playing in the white Florida sand of the streets smoke. They are little nicotine volcanoes. A chubby, olive faced urchin with a six-inch weed, which is known popularly in Ybor City as a *caballo muerto* ('dead horse'), is a sight so frequent as to attract little attention beyond an indolent 'bravo.'" (*New York Herald*, quoted in *Tampa Tribune*, February 14, 1890)

"Many of the cheaper cigars are made in small household factories known as 'buck-eyes' or *chinchales* (bedbugs). In these a section of a cottage is separated from the living quarters by chicken wire in order to conform to government regulations. Every member of the family helps in the rolling and packing of cigars." (Federal Writers' Project, 1941)

"How I love the wit of cigar makers! That word *chinchal*, for example. It comes from the Spanish word for bedbugs which is *chinches* and so *chinchal* is a place where bedbugs gather and as you can imagine they do not need much space." (Jose Yglesias, 1971)

The owner of a buckeye (chinchal) *with a group of cigar makers.*

"Small factories, where the owner also does practically all of the work, frequently are located in one end of a building or the back room of a residence. These are known as 'buckeyes' or *chinchales*. The latter . . . becomes a plain *chinch* in English." (Federal Writers' Project, 1938)

"Ybor City, it was like the frontier. Husbands say their wives don't work, but women always work. Like my mother, she raised eight children. Grandma and two cousins also lived in the house. We got a duplex, there were so many people. . . . Laundry, so much laundry. And cooking, of course. She even kept a vegetable garden to help out. . . . Yes, and in the buckeye, the *chinchal*. . . . She worked there a lot, especially in slow times or when workers were hard to get." (Dolores Río, 1985)

"I was fifteen in 1929 when I learned to make cigars. . . . It takes you a year to learn that as an *aprendiz,* an apprentice. . . . I went to a buckeye, a *chinchal,* in Palmetto Beach [south of Ybor City]. This man we knew had a little shop with about fifteen or twenty cigar makers. I learned to roll cigars." (Dalia Corro, 2002)

A chinchal in Ybor City.

La Flora cigar factory (1909), located on Ninth Avenue and Twentieth Street, was owned by Pedro Casellas, who used his chinchal as a school to train young cigar makers.

Pedro Casellas.

"The immigrant coming to Tampa is surrounded by people of his own nationality, speaking the same language. The result is that today in Tampa ninety-eight percent of the cigar makers talk Spanish, and mighty few speak English. They have the same habits and live precisely as they did in the mother country." (*Cigar Makers' Official Journal*, December 1909)

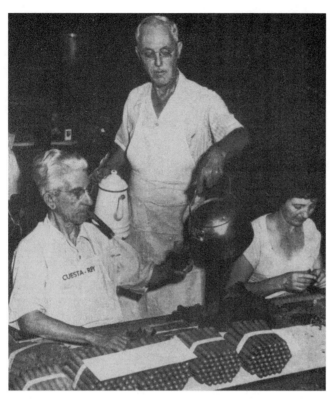

*Manuel García Alonso, el Cafetero, dispensing coffee at the Cuesta-Rey factory.
(Courtesy of Willie García)*

"Every cigar factory had a *Cafetero*. He was awarded a concession by the factory
owners to deliver coffee to the employees at their work stations. My father, Manuel
García Alonso, was *el Cafetero* for Cuesta-Rey cigar factory at Beach Street and
Howard Avenue in West Tampa. He became a partner with Fuentes Iglesias in 1923
and sole proprietor in 1927. He operated the business until retiring in 1955. His Atlanta
Restaurant was in a building owned by the factory owners and located across Beach
Street from the factory. . . . At the restaurant, the coffee was brewed for delivery to the
workers. My father took the coffee three times a day—early morning, mid-morning
and mid-afternoon. He had two large coffee pots, one for the boiled milk and one for
the black Cuban coffee. He provided the workers with enameled metal cups which
they kept at their work stations. . . . All of the sales were on credit. On Saturday the
workers were paid in cash. *El Cafetero* would set up a table at the front entrance and
collect for the weekly sales. I always marveled at how my father could remember each
worker's charges—there were several hundred of them—without the benefit of books
or written accounts. When a worker would question my father's total, he would re-
mind them of the day that they had had an extra cup of coffee." (Willie García, 1997)

"The factories were as much fun as a carnival; there were always lots of peddlers
coming in selling hot *bollos* (pea-meal fritters), *empanadas* (small meat pies), *pirulis*
(candy suckers), and all kinds of sweets." (Norerto Díaz, 1942)

"The old institution whereby one man read while others applied their fingers to the fashioning of cigars originated in Cuba almost with the birth of the cigar industry, according to men who are old-timers in the industry." (*Tampa Morning Tribune*, September 27, 1926)

"Upon entering one of the large manufacturing rooms in which some two hundred men were seated at their tables making cigars [at the Ybor factory], the first thing that attracted our attention was a gentleman seated upon an elevated platform in the middle of the room reading in a loud voice—of course it was in their native tongue. This we were told is their custom in all the factories. He read regularly every day for the benefit of all and is paid by the operatives. We found the same thing in the ladies' department, only a lady was reading." (*Orlando Sentinel*, quoted in *Tampa Tribune*, July 5, 1888)

"The hands in the cigar rooms follow the time honored Cuban custom and employ a *lector*, or reader, who from a pulpit in the geometrical center of the apartment entertains his auditors with the latest Havana newspapers in the morning and with Spanish novels and ballads in the afternoon." (*New York Herald*, quoted in *Tampa Tribune*, February 14, 1890)

A reader (lector) in a Havana cigar factory (c. 1890).

"The *lectura* was itself a veritable system of education dealing with a variety of subjects, including politics, labor, literature, and international relations. We had four daily shifts (*turnos*). One was used to read national news stories. Another was devoted to international political developments. The third concerned itself entirely with news from the proletariat press. And, lastly, the novel." (Abelardo Gutiérrez Días, 1975)

"Whenever we finished one novel, a list with a few names of different books was passed around, and the cigar makers would vote for the one they wanted. The book with the majority vote is the one that was read next." (Wilfredo Rodríguez, 1981)

"Almost all the novels chosen were by Spanish authors like Armando Palacio Valdés and Pérez Galdós. Emile Zola also enjoyed enormous popularity among the workers. At the beginning, almost all the novels involved serious themes, usually labor-related subjects—that was at a time when the factories were made up almost entirely of men. Afterwards, during the late 1920s, women entered the factories in increasing numbers. And through the very force of the women's vote, we began to read more romantic novels." (Abelardo Gutiérrez Días, 1975)

A lector reading to cigar makers in the Cuesta-Rey factory (1929).

The staff of La Traducción, *an Ybor City newspaper, in the 1936.*

"The difficulty of providing sufficient Spanish-language reading material for the *lector* was remedied when *lector* Ramón Valdespino began to publish, with the aid of a typewriter and a mimeograph machine, a seven- or eight-page newspaper in which the telegraphic dispatches and articles of greatest interest appearing the day before, or the same day, in the *Tampa Tribune* and the *Tampa Journal* were translated into Spanish. Valdespino used as title of his original newspaper *La Traducción* (The Translation). The reading of *La Traducción* expanded into all the cigar factories of Tampa. The newspaper was published without any change to its original format for more than twenty years." (José Rivero Muñiz, 1958)

"There is an association of cigar factory readers in this city, maintaining offices in Ybor City. . . . At this office, all night long, a force of interpreters is at work, translating from New York papers, from magazines and from Tampa papers news and articles to be read in the factories the next day. Copies are made of the stories thus selected from a considerable range of publications, in multiple, and are supplied to each of the factories. But the readers are not dependent alone upon news translated from English—extracts are taken from some of the Havana papers and thus distributed, and the readers also read from newspapers and books published in Spanish. . . . In some factories, there are readers among the packers, as well as among the cigar makers." (*Tampa Daily Times*, September 20, 1914)

"*El lector* had to be an educated man to make the translation from English to Spanish. . . . In the first period, we read political news from the world over. In the second period, we read news from labor organizations, also the world over. In the third and fourth periods, we read history, novels, culture, entertainment. The great *Don Quixote* by Cervantes was a favorite. We were more than readers. We also actors. We read in character. We read to make the characters come alive. We were performers." (Honorato Henry Domínguez, 1977)

"In those days we didn't use any microphones. . . . You had to have a strong voice and very clear pronunciation so the workers understand every word you read. . . . It was exactly like the theater. When we were reading a novel we were to make ourselves as though we were the character who was talking—whether it was a woman or a child, an old man or an old lady. Not everybody could do that." (Wilfredo Rodríguez, 1981)

"The workers were the ones who decided who would be the *lectores,* not the owners of the factory. If the *lector* didn't read what they wanted or didn't read with the right kind of emotion, they would vote him out and get another one." (César Medina, 1982)

Joaquín de la Llana, known as "El Conde" (the Count), was a native of Asturias, Spain, and worked as a lector in Ybor City during the 1920s. (Courtesy of Judy Deese)

Luisa Capetillo, a Puerto Rican and one of the few women to serve as a reader in Tampa, was photographed in Havana in 1915, two years after she briefly worked in Ybor City. (Courtesy of University of Puerto Rico Libraries)

"I am a socialist because I want all the advances, discoveries and inventions to belong to everyone, and that socialization be established without privileges. Some want a state to regulate it; I want it without government. . . . I stick to my position as a decided partisan of no government: anarchist socialism. . . . Brotherhood as the supreme law, without frontiers or divisions of race, color, or language, will be established as the religious ideal in schools. . . . Don't take woman as a mere object of pleasure; respect in her the mother of the human race. . . . Saturated as I was by the ills of society, I had no trouble exposing the crimes and vices that this bundle of stupidities inflicts on women." (Luisa Capetillo, 1911)

"A fatal duel with pistols occurred this morning at 9 o'clock, at the corner of Eighteenth Street and Ninth Avenue, between Jesus Fernández, a Spaniard, and Enrique Velásquez, a Mexican. . . . A peculiar feature of the case is that the trouble which resulted in the fatal affray arose from a discussion of a novel. . . . For some time there has existed a bitter controversy in the José Lovera cigar factory, the question being whether or not the reader of the factory should read from his stand to the operatives the novel *La Canaille* by the French author, Emile Zola. A number of the female employees of the factory objected to the Zola story being read, claiming that it was obscene and unfit for the ears of a woman. Many of the men, however, desired the book read, and, being in the majority, brought the question to a vote of the employees. A majority vote was cast in favor of reading the book. In the hot discussion attendant upon the question, Jesus Fernández and Enrique Velásquez, who had been friends, fell out, and championed opposite sides. Saturday night, the two men met and came to blows on the issue as to the obscenity or purity of *La Canaille*. . . . Yesterday morning, they met again and immediate action followed. After exchanging a word or two, Fernández drew a 38-caliber pistol and Velásquez likewise produced a 44-caliber pistol. They opened fire when they were in arm's length of each other." (*Tampa Morning Tribune*, December 22, 1904)

"Enrique Velásquez, the Mexican who was reported dead yesterday afternoon, from the effects of the street duel yesterday morning, revived and rested quietly last night." (*Tampa Morning Tribune*, December 23, 1904)

Tampa cigar makers listening to a reader (upper right). (Courtesy of Florida State Archives)

A lector *reading to cigar makers (1930).*

"The *lector* . . . did not have the benefit of a loudspeaker system. It was all through the strength of one's voice (*fuerzo de grito*). In one factory, such as the Martínez Ybor factory which contained some 300 cigar workers, one had to read loud enough to be heard by everyone. It was an enormous effort. One enterprising *lector,* seeking to improve the system and thereby make his life easier, introduced into the factory a loudspeaker. But the *lector*'s voice through the megaphone annoyed the majority of workers; it was too metallic, they complained. In deference to the workers' protest, the *lector* abandoned the loudspeaker." (Abelardo Gutiérrez Días, 1975)

"I used to walk by [the Corral-Wodiska factory] and my father would be reading. All the windows would be open and I could listen to him reading the novel. It was like a soap opera. When he got to that crucial moment in the story, he'd stop and close the book. And, I could hear everybody go 'ahhh.' . . . The reader was the prince of the factory. Cigar workers came to work at 6 or 7 o'clock; the reader picked his own time of arrival. When the cigar worker was making $10 or $12 a week, the reader could make up to $60 or $70." (Henry Aparicio, 1981)

Cigar makers at the Corral-Wodiska factory (1929), listening to a lector *(upper right).*

"The reader's salary was negotiated by a committee of workers headed by *el presidente de la lectura* (president of the reading). In most cases, the quota was fixed at twenty-five cents a week per worker. . . . Besides helping select materials to be read and collecting the workers' contribution to the reader, the president was also responsible for keeping time. He was the one who rang the bell for the reader to start reading and for the reader to finish. The president would also rattle his bell whenever the level of laughter or 'noise' interfered with the reading." (*Tampa Times,* May 22, 1981)

"If a reader's performance was worthy of extraordinary recognition, a worker simply tapped his knife (*chaveta*), with which he was cutting tobacco, on his bench." (Hermann G. Stelzner and Danio Bazo, 1965)

"The black Cuban community was very proud of the only black *lector,* Facundo Acción, who carried himself with great dignity. He was, without question, the black Cuban community's recognized leading intellectual." (Evelio Grillo, 2000)

A demonstration by Ybor City cigar workers in support of a strike (c. 1899).

"The Havana manufacturers who had begun the cigar industry in Key West . . . set up a company town in Tampa to get their businesses away from the ferment in Key West, but there too the fervor for Cuban independence was accompanied by strikes for higher wages, a closed shop, sometimes simply for a better grade outer leaf for the cigars they made. The manufacturers were in the main Spanish and they seemed at a loss to diagnose the fever that swept their workers everywhere. They were as ignorant as the medical scientists of the day: In Key West (and then in Tampa) the manufacturers had imported from Havana the skilled workers necessary to make luxury cigars in this new uninfected island, and when the same malady broke out there, they did not know what sea wind had carried the seeds from Cuba." (Jose Yglesias, 1971)

"Unions, international and local, representing every occupation known to the cigar industry, singly and in groups, sprang into being as laborers increased in number. In time the manufacturers had to suffer not only for their own sins but for the jealousies and strife among the unions themselves. . . . Naturally strikes, some of them very bitter and of long duration, were often the results of these conditions." (U.S. Immigration Commission, 1911)

"Thirteen weeks ago there was a strike at the Ybor-Manrara factory because the cigar makers objected to the firm weighing the [tobacco for] fillers. . . . They struck, and as weeks rolled on, the men began to show restlessness in other factories, and it was feared by other manufacturers that more trouble would ensue if the strike [against Ybor-Manrara] was not broken. . . . Last week a meeting of manufacturers was held, and it was decided to organize [a lockout of cigar workers] for protection against this labor trouble, and to end the strike." (*Tobacco*, July 14, 1899)

"The laborer insists that he has as much right to dictate the terms of his labor as the capitalist has to manage his own affairs. It is nonsense for the cigar manufacturers to attempt to treat intelligent cigar makers like a lot of slaves." (Anonymous letter, *Tampa Morning Tribune*, August 9, 1899)

"During this strike thousands of cigar makers left for New York, Key West, and Cuba. I also left for Cuba with my wife and children. In August of the same year, my wife returned with the children. I, myself, came back the following week. We found that we could no longer endure life in Cuba as we had become accustomed to a life of comfort and ease in Ybor City which we could not find in Cuba." (José Ramón Sanfeliz, 1936)

"Vamos a pescar jaibas" (Let's go fish for crabs). A group of striking cigar makers on an outing during the 1899 Weight Strike.

A soup kitchen set up in Ybor City to feed striking cigar workers in 1899.

"The locked out men are taking matters as cooly as they can, and are doing all they can to prevent suffering in their ranks. Free soup houses have been established in West Tampa, Port Tampa City, and on Eighth Avenue in Ybor City. An average of one thousand a day have been fed free so far." (*Tobacco*, July 28, 1899)

"The result of the Tampa strike furnishes a splendid illustration of what unity of action and oneness of purpose can accomplish. Twenty of the large manufacturers locked out about 4,000 cigar makers in order to force the cigar makers to accept work in a factory that was on strike. This action on the part of the employers completely tied up the cigar industry of Tampa, but instead of having the effect desired and confidently expected by the employers, the locked-out men got together and formulated a new scale of prices that advanced wages in some cases $15. They adopted shop rules. Every one of the demands of the strikers were conceded by the employers. They are as follows: (1) The abolition of the scales. (2) A uniform scale of prices for all grades of cigars. (3) Supplies of water to be kept constantly on hand for the use of the men. (4) Factories to be scrubbed and cleaned once a month. (4) That coal be used for fuel instead of wood in winter months. (5) Right of the cigar makers' central committee at any time to inspect any factory to see that these regulations are carried out." (*Cigar Makers' Official Journal*, September 1899)

"When in 1902 I landed in Tampa, I found myself in a world of radicals for which I was prepared. In those days in Tampa, anarchists and socialists were many." (Angelo Massari, 1965)

"Let me say it right out—Ybor City was a radical, trade-union town. . . . [Cigar workers] kept alive the Cuban revolutionary tradition (José Martí gave some of his most important political speeches there) and also the Spanish and Italian anarchist ones." (Jose Yglesias, 1977)

Angelo Massari (1903), an Italian immigrant, who worked as a cigar maker in Ybor City.

La Federación, *"the official paper of Tampa's cigar makers, selectors, and pickers,"* was published from 1899 to 1901.

"The organization of labor that is not planted squarely on the class struggle can develop only in one direction—the direction of a buffer for the capitalist class, run by Labor Lieutenants of Capital." (*La Federación*, December 14, 1900)

"After many short strikes and conflict among ourselves, we decided to create a strong organization as the only means by which to bring order to the existing confusion and to obtain a wage that would allow us to live with dignity and tranquility. But the divisions that existed among the cigar workers were so great that many times we doubted that we would achieve our goals. . . . Finally, we decided to organize and gave ourselves the name Resistencia. We respected the Cigar Makers' International Union and at first we all got along. But we soon realized that it did not respect us. It was useless. The war thus began." (Luis Barcia Quilabert, 1957)

"There is a movement on foot by the Resistencia Union to gobble up everything pertaining to the cigar manufacturing interest. . . . They have gathered in all the members of the International Cigar Makers' Union, and if they succeed in getting the box makers to join them, they will about have things their own way." (*United States Tobacco Journal*, June 8, 1901)

THE MORNING TRIBUNE.

THE TRIBUNE IS THE ONLY MORNING PAPER PUBLISHED IN TAMPA, AND ITS TELEGRAPHIC SERVICE COVERS THE FIELD THOROUGHLY

TAMPA FLORIDA SATURDAY JULY 27 1901

GENERAL STRIKE IS ON TODAY; FIVE THOUSAND WORKERS IDLE

Cigar Manufacturing Industry To Be Again Tied Up. Resistencia Quits Work In a Body.   Demands Were Not Granted. Strike Thus Far Has Been Peacefully Effected.

"With three exceptions every cigar factory in Tampa is closed. The general strike commenced, and how long it will last is problematical. The workmen are expressing themselves as confident they will win, but they are making preparations for a long struggle. . . . The workmen have a fund of $32,000." (Tobacco Leaf, July 31, 1901)

"About the only thing that has occurred during the past week worthy of comment was the mysterious way in which the most blatant of the Resistencia leaders disappeared." (*Tobacco Leaf,* August 14, 1901)

"Tampa is in a great stew. . . . A strike was ordered . . . [and] unable to settle the difference peaceably, the businessmen of that city are now kidnapping the leaders of the strike and taking them away—the public knows not where." (*Weekly Tallahasseean,* August 8, 1901)

AGITATORS ABDUCTED BY BUSINESS MEN

Citizens of Tampa, Fla., Determined to Get Rid of Professional Labor Leaders.

SEIZED THEM AT NIGHT

Shipped Thirteen on a Schooner Bound for Honduras, and Hunted for More.

TAMPA, Fla., Wednesday.—With thirteen of its leaders kidnapped by business men of this city, La Resistencia, the local union of cigarmakers, which has six thousand men and women members, is like a headless giant. The organization seems to be in a sort of stupor. Lacking the directing brains which have conducted its business, it is inactive and uncertain what to do.

New York Herald, *August 8, 1901.*

"Governor of the State of Florida: The undersigned appeal to you, as the only representative of justice in this State, and kindly ask of you to do all you can in our behalf. Since the 5ᵗʰ [of August] our husbands were outrageously kidnapped from homes, and their whereabouts are not known to us. . . . Their only guilt is that they're strikers, who have as all the rest, demanded from the Cigar Manufacturers what is just and equitable. There were no warrants issued for their arrest as it is customary, in all cases, but [they] were ignominiously kidnapped from our homes, and on the streets by the police, contrary to the laws of any civilized country. Why are they not brought before a magistrate and judged? It seems to us that prejudice prevails against them. Therefore, Hon. Sir, all we ask is justice, and if same exists then let us have the benefit of same."
(Isabel Otero, Loretta Casellas, and Carolina Barcia, August 12, 1901)

A letter sent to the governor from the wives of three kidnapped strikers.

THE MORNING TRIBUNE.

THE TRIBUNE IS THE ONLY MORNING PAPER PUBLISHED IN TAMPA, AND ITS TELEGRAPHIC SERVICE COVERS THE FIELD THOROUGHLY

TAMPA. FLORIDA. FRIDAY. AUGUST 23. 1901

MARIE COOPER ARRIVED LAST NIGHT AT MIDNIGHT; LANDED AGITATORS IN HONDURAS

"At a few minutes before midnight last night, the auxiliary schooner *Marie Cooper* steamed into the Hillsborough River . . . with a cargo of coconuts, from Bonaco, Honduras. On board . . . were the eight guards who had charge of the thirteen deported agitators, who were shipped out of Tampa on the *Marie Cooper,* from Ballast Point, on Wednesday morning, August 7. . . . The *Cooper* had a fair voyage all the way to the shores of Honduras. . . . The prisoners on board . . . were landed on a desolate beach. . . . They were given a parting admonition. . . . 'Be seen again in Tampa, and it means death,' said the guards to the thirteen castaways." (*Tampa Morning Tribune,* August 23, 1901)

"The only consolation that will console our disappeared (*desaparecidos*) comrades is the idea that the ones they left behind, raise the flag of right and justice. . . . Forward comrades! Long live solidarity!" (Resistencia "MANIFESTO," August 1901)

"The striking cigar makers are keeping very quiet, and with only one exception are not even making any inflammable speeches. That exception is a woman named Luise Herrera, who is the secretary of the Resistencia Strippers' Union. Whenever and wherever she can secure an audience of cigar makers, she delivers herself of the most vituperative language against the manufacturers and especially the committee of citizens who rid Tampa of her brother Anarchists." (*United States Tobacco Journal,* August 24, 1901)

"The longest and most serious strike in the history of Tampa's cigar industry was terminated yesterday officially by the Resistencia union. A general meeting of the union was held at the Resistencia headquarters on Seventh Avenue. Over a thousand members of the various branches of the union, representing selectors, pickers, packers, strippers and cigar makers, were present. . . . It was shown that the funds were exhausted, that the men were more or less anxious to get back to work. . . . A resolution declaring the strike at an end was unanimously carried. . . . The strike just ended went into effect on July 26. . . . The men returned to work under the terms proposed by the manufacturers. All the factories are in the future to be open factories, and no union is to be recognized inside the houses." (*Tampa Morning Tribune*, November 24, 1901)

"In 1901 we lost the strike and that was bitter, bitter. The committee, seeing that we could not win and knowing the hunger there was, called a meeting to recommend that we go back to work. Who would tell the workers this? So we asked Romalla, the reader at our factory, to give the speech, for he was a master of the emotions. I had not cried before but I cried then—though I was on the committee and knew what he was going to say. . . . Romalla ended his speech by saying, '*Nos han vencido pero no convencido!*'—They have vanquished us but not convinced us. And we went back to work believing that." ("Estefano Scolaro," 1971)

Cigar makers in Tampa (c. 1910).

"[After the 1901 strike] La Resistencia declined in importance, and was eventually replaced by the Cigar Makers' International Union (CMIU)." (Stetson Kennedy, 1942)

"Today there are about 7,500 cigar makers, packers and selectors in [Tampa]. . . . We have all told organized 5,540. . . . The condition of cigar makers during the last ten years has gone from bad to worse. . . . Skilled Clear Havana Spanish style workmen are receiving less in wages in Tampa today than the average cigar maker receives . . . in the [CMIU] organized cities. Most of them realize now that they are doing this because of lack of organization." (*Cigar Makers' Official Journal*, December 1909)

"The second general strike in Tampa cigar factories occurred June 25, 1910, and continued until January 26, 1911. It was conducted by the Cigar Makers' International Union. The cause of this strike may be traced to the noncompliance of certain manufacturers with the equalization of prices [for making cigars]." (A. Stuart Campbell, 1939)

TAMPA MORNING TRIBUNE

FULL ASSOCIATED PRESS REPORT BY LEASED WIRE SERVICE

TAMPA, FLORIDA   WEDNESDAY, SEPTEMBER 21, 1910   TWELVE PAGES

TWO MEN TAKEN FROM OFFICERS, AND HANGED

Castange Ficcarotta and Angelo Albano Victims of Lynch Law While Being Transferred to County Jail By Officers

During the 1910 strike, unknown vigilantes lynched two Italian immigrants, Angelo Albano and Castenge Ficarrotta, who were already in police custody, accused of murdering a cigar factory employee.

"Following the murder of J. F. Easterling, a bookkeeper, at the Bustillo factory in West Tampa, local citizens became aroused and an unknown group of lynchers took the lives of two Italians who were allegedly guilty of the crime." (A. Stuart Campbell, 1939)

"Neither Ficcarrotta nor Albano were directly connected with the strike of cigar makers." (*Tampa Morning Tribune*, September 22, 1910)

"What occurred in West Tampa causes deep sadness . . . because it clearly reveals what our enemies are capable of doing to defeat us." (*El Internacional* [Tampa], September 23, 1910)

"For six months the Tampa lockout and strike with all its attendant startling episodes, has continued, and under conditions the like of which has never occurred in any other place." (*Cigar Makers' Official Journal*, December 1910)

"The sturdy and determined citizenry of Tampa asserted itself. The people who have built up this city and who have protected its interests and its welfare in the past are not to be found wanting at this critical juncture. They have served notice that the control and direction of this community is to be retained by its law-abiding, representative and reputable citizens—and that its future is not to be blasted through the malevolent combination of the hired assassin and the transient agitator." (*Tampa Morning Tribune*, September 22, 1910)

"From the opinion of the Italian colony at Tampa and from the result of my inquiry, I have reason to believe that the lynching itself was not the outcome of a temporary outburst of popular anger, but was rather planned, in cold blood, to the most trifling detail, by some citizens of West Tampa with the tacit assent of a few police officers, and all with the intention of teaching an awful lesson to the strikers of the cigar factories." (G. Moroni, 1910)

Lynchers placed a pipe mockingly in the mouth of one victim (left) and attached a note to the feet of the other victim, reading: "Beware! Others take notice or go the same way. We know even more. We are watching you. If any more citizens are molested, look out."

Members of the Cigar Makers' International Union at Tampa's Labor Day parade in 1912, the year after they were defeated in the strike that lasted seven months.

"During the long strike, workers received financial help from their fellow workers in Cuba and from the International Union until its funds were exhausted. The strike leaders decided to organize a referendum among the workers to determine whether to continue the strike or return to work. Upon the majority voting in favor of returning to work, the factories reopened their doors and work resumed. Many of the families that had sought refuge in Cuba when the conflict began subsequently returned to Tampa." (José Rivero Muñiz, 1958)

"Labor must Organize to successfully cope with Organized Capital. . . . The rich meet in club or parlor. Working men, when they combine, gather in the street. All the organized forces of society are against them. Capital has the army and the navy, the legislature, the judicial and executive departments." (*El Internacional* [Tampa], March 31, 1911)

"At the factory of Celestino Vega & Co., the workers refused to walk out [during a 1916 strike], and the strikers rushed into the factory deriding and hooting the workers. It is reported that the women leading the mob called the men at work 'females' and offered their skirts to those who refused to quit. By request of Mr. Vega, two special policemen were stationed at the factory today to prevent recurrence of this disorder." (*Tobacco Leaf,* November 16, 1916)

"Sweethearts, wives, and daughters of union men are invited to meet the union women of Tampa at Carpenter's Hall on February 28. What is planned is a grand reorganization of the Women's Union Label League." (*El Internacional* [Tampa], February 24, 1911)

Tampa cigar makers (c. 1920). (Courtesy of John S. Favata)

A bunch maker working with a mold.

"The hand mold process of cigar-making originated in an effort to improve on the productivity of the Spanish hand system. Molds first came into use in the . . . last century, but their use was not widespread until after 1910. They were used then in Tampa to a considerable extent and proved popular, the manufacturers liking the lower cost of production which they permitted, and the workers their higher earnings with them. In the mold process the cigar makers work in teams of three, one bunch maker and two rollers. The bunch maker keeps the two rollers supplied with bunches and they put on the wrappers. The bunch maker places a special binder leaf around the filler to form the bunch, binders being necessary with molds. Then, as each bunch is finished, he inserts it into a mold. This device consists of two wooden blocks in which cigar shaped receptacles have been carved. . . . After the bunches have been placed in the molds . . . a top is placed over them and pressure applied in a mold press." (A. Stuart Campbell, 1939)

A bunch maker tightening a press to hold the two sides of the mold in place.

Cigar makers (c. 1930) using molds, which are stacked in the presses that appear in the left and right foreground.

"Mold workers work in teams, thereby creating a rivalry between the bunch maker and wrapper roller. If either gets behind, the other calls him to task, and . . . the records will show that the mold workers are making a better average wage than the hand workers, not because they are better paid, but because they work." (*Tobacco Leaf*, November 30, 1916)

"There is a great change in the trade here in Tampa, for five years ago there was mostly all clear Havana hand work, but now it is mostly all team work, and it seems like all shops are having mold work done." (*Cigar Makers' Official Journal*, December 1919)

The lodge of Caballeros de la Luz (Knights of the Light), a Cuban fraternal and mutual aid society, was located on Seventh Avenue in the 1890s.

"When we got to this country, we had to take care of ourselves. No one else would do it for us. These clubs provided a kind of hospitalization insurance that was unheard of in the old days. And they were more than that—they were social clubs with all kinds of activities." (Manuel Tamargo, 1977)

"I intend . . . to describe Ybor City as the visitor sees it at night—a veritable Havana. . . . When night comes, and the electric light illuminates the whole place with a silvery halo of great beauty and a high degree of intensity, the cafés and other public resorts fill up with the cigar makers who now indulge in a perfect fusillade of conversation, card-playing and other amusements. As can be seen there, the Cubans are a very sociable people among themselves, and extremely polite to and friendly with strangers. . . . The interior of many of the places of public resort are very fine—handsomely fitted up and attractive in the unrestricted use of that word. . . . Many of the private residences are furnished elegantly, and at night the Cubans' fondness for music, and sociability, can be noticed in the many strains of music coming from pianos, guitars, and other instruments, manipulated by talented and expert musicians." (*Tampa Daily Journal,* March 5, 1890)

The first clubhouse of the Centro Español on Seventh Avenue was officially dedicated in 1892.

"The Centro Español's first building was a large frame structure with two towers, containing a theater, dance hall, canteen, soda fountain and classrooms costing $16,000, which put the club considerably in debt. A Spanish Casino Stock Company was organized to give theatrical productions in the club's theater. . . . Operas, dramas, and vaudeville were given in Spanish, and the theater paid a handsome profit." (Federal Writers' Project, 1937)

"What brought about the founding of the Centro Español was . . . the necessity of mutual protection of the Spaniards. . . . The Spaniards at that time were persecuted, abhorred and were the target of the Cuban hatred because of the Spanish government in Cuba. The persecution was so intensive that even their right to live was made difficult." (B. M. Balbotín, 1936)

"It was erected firstly to unite the Spanish colony of Tampa, and secondly to create a center for recreation and instruction. It is our intention to have familiar gatherings once a week and classes in the English and Spanish languages. Instruction will be given in the branches of literature and science, so that this may become to its members a temple of learning, wisdom and honor." (Ignacio Haya, 1892)

"The Centro Español long ago proved that little men of humble means can enjoy life to the brim simply by pooling resources for the common good. That obvious truth prompted the little band of cigar makers to organize in September of 1891 the tiny organization from which sprang the benevolent Centro of today, catering to the medical and recreational needs of 6,000 members." (*Tampa Daily Times*, December 10, 1941)

"The average man in Ybor City hardly ever stayed home at night. As soon as he got through dinner, he generally went to the clubs, where they had coffee and played dominoes and discussed politics and that went on day in day out, and that was true among the Spaniards, the Italians, and the Cubans." (César Medina, 1988)

Located on Seventh Avenue and dedicated in 1912, this building of the Centro Español, which members used until 1983, included a theater, ballroom, and canteen with a bar.

Laying the cornerstone of the Centro Español hospital located on Tampa's Bayshore Boulevard, August 25, 1904.

"Cooperative social medicine societies were established by the Tampa Latins as early as 1887 and have flourished ever since. Presumably they were the first such organizations in the United States and have remained in continuous operation longer than any others in this country." (Stetson Kennedy, 1942)

"The clubs provided complete medical service for members for a small weekly or monthly fee. These services included clinics, doctors, medicines and hospitals. . . . The medical services provided by the clubs were labeled socialistic and were strongly opposed by the local medical association." (Braulio Alonso, 1997)

"Cooperative medical service was launched in Tampa . . . before 'socialized medicine' became a controversial national issue. Soon after the cigar industry migrated to Tampa in 1886, a Cuban physician, Dr. Guillermo Machado, was conducting a mutual benefit society for medical aid. For ten cents a week, members of *La Iguala* (The Equal) were entitled to medicine and services. . . . In 1906 the Central Español erected a $60,000 hospital where members could obtain medical care and hospitalization in return for their dues of $1.50 a week." (Federal Writers' Project, 1939)

Almost two years in the making, the Sanatorio del Centro Español opened in 1906.

"Members of the working class, in the early days, became dissatisfied with . . . what some considered the unreasonable attitude of officials [of the Centro Español]. They brought into existence a new club for those of more modest circumstances. A large body of the Centro Español members seceded in 1902 and formed the Centro Asturiano." (Federal Writers' Project, 1937)

"Centro Asturiano was mainly for the Spaniards who came from the province of Asturias, in northern Spain. Centro Español was for all the rest of the Spaniards. Always, the Asturians and others from the northern provinces have considered themselves a separate country. I guess our pride, maybe our stubbornness, made us have one for just ourselves." (Manuel Tamargo, 1977)

"El Centro Asturiano is affiliated with the parent society in Cuba. . . . Its casino, or club house, has a library of Spanish, French, and English standard works, a theater where local talent disports itself for the amusement of members and their friends, pool rooms, a gymnasium, and a café and bar. . . . The society has 3,500 members, while its buildings, land, and furnishings are worth about $200,000." (U.S. Immigration Commission, 1911)

The original clubhouse of the Centro Asturiano on Seventh Avenue served as home of the organization, chartered in 1902, until it burned down in 1912. Membership records from April 1902 show the names of many cigar workers.

The current building of Centro Asturiano was dedicated in 1914. This 1926 view includes a sign in Spanish (left) announcing "Today—Debut of the Notable Spanish Baritone José Abella in 'Los Molinos de Viento.'"

"The club is not only the center of social activities, but also is a haven for the tired workers who are confined throughout the day in cigar factories. When the day's work is done, the workers may take advantage of the gymnasium and pool, and afterwards spend their time in the reading room or the pool room. The attractiveness of this feature is shown by the crowd that fills the big structure every day of the week. Membership also provides medical attention in case of sickness and even treatment in the sanatorium. There are classes in English for the Spanish and classes in Spanish for the English-speaking. The institution also has a banking department." (*Tampa Daily Times,* December 14, 1922)

"I remember going to the Centro Asturiano on Saturdays to become more proficient in Spanish." (Braulio Alonso, 1997)

The Sanatorio del Centro Asturiano in Ybor City was built at a cost of $15,000 and dedicated in 1905.

"Its sanatorium, or hospital, has accommodations for 100 patients in the general ward and for about 35 patients who may be suffering from contagious diseases in isolated wards." (U.S. Immigration Commission, 1911)

"The Asturians deserve the credit for launching social medicine on a large scale in Tampa. After seceding from the Centro Español, they . . . [constructed] the first social medicine to be built in the United States, its facilities the most modern available." (Stetson Kennedy, 1942)

"At the end of the [Cuban War of Independence] . . . the Cuban residents of Tampa, desirous of having a place to gather and continue their social activities, organized a recreational society which was called Club Nacional Cubano, situated on Fourteenth Street and Ninth Avenue. The club was inaugurated the 10th day of October 1899, with a reception and dance." (Federal Writers' Project, 1937)

"In 1902 the name of the club was changed to the Círculo Cubano. At present there are 500 members of this club, composed of all nationalities and classes, the Cubans, however, being in great majority. . . . The new building of the Círculo Cubano is situated at the corner of Tenth Avenue and Fourteenth Street and was built in 1907. . . . The building is made of brick and is two stories, containing a theater, club rooms, school rooms, pool rooms and café. The theater has a seating capacity of 1,500. . . . It is the custom of the society to give its members one or two free theatrical performances monthly and also a dance whenever the occasion calls for one." (*Tampa Morning Tribune,* May 23, 1909)

The original clubhouse of the Círculo Cubano (Cuban Club) in Ybor City was built in 1907 at a cost of $18,000; it burned down in 1916.

Laying the cornerstone of the current Cuban Club in 1917.

"As [the members of the Círculo Cubano] could count on the $35,000 loan [toward the estimated cost of $65,000], it was necessary to raise the rest of the sum to finish the job. They floated an issue of $20 and $5 bonds which were sold among the members. A sum of $10,000 was raised from these bonds. Besides this, they organized a series of festivals to which the people of Tampa responded as a whole." (Federal Writers' Project, 1937)

"The Club had to buy all the furniture for every department, but there was no money with which to buy it. . . . For this purpose a bazaar was held at the Sans Souci Theatre on Seventh Avenue. . . . This bazaar lasted eight days, during which time an orchestra played Cuban, Spanish and American music. Lunches were served as well as drinks. The different objects that the members donated were raffled by means of roulette, producing at this festival a considerable monetary aid. . . . During this campaign to raise funds, the athletic division began to give exhibitions of amateur boxing in the gymnasium. . . . Plays are presented in the club's theater, dances given in its ballroom, and indoor games enjoyed in its recreational rooms. In some years the membership has reached 2,500." (Federal Writers' Project, 1937)

The Cuban Club building that was dedicated in 1918 and still stands.

"I was one of the founders of the Club Nacional Cubano (Cuban National Club), today known as the Cuban Club. This predecessor of the Cuban Club was composed of white or black members—a sort of rice with black beans. There was no distinction of races. When the Círculo Cubano (Cuban Club) was formed [in 1902], however, the Negroes were left out. These Negroes then formed their own club which is called Club Martí-Maceo." (José Ramón Sanfeliz, 1936)

"Black Cubans worked in the factories alongside white Cubans. While my mother formed interracial relationships at work, few, if any, such friendships extended to visits in the homes. . . . Black Cubans had their own mutual benefit society and social center, La Unión Martí-Maceo. . . . Black Cubans and white Cubans interacted in the streets and in public places, such as grocery stores, produce stands, meat markets, and in the corner saloon, where men who were not at work gathered in the afternoon. . . . Blacks and whites also belonged to the same grocery cooperative and to the same prepay health clinic. . . . With the exception of the local corner bar, which they could patronize, black Cubans did not share recreational activities with white Cubans." (Evelio Grillo, 2000)

The founders of La Unión Martí-Maceo, a mutual aid society created by black Cubans in 1904.

The original building of La Unión Martí-Maceo.

"The government told [black and white Cubans] we could not work together, have a society together, and would have to keep the races apart. That was the law of the country. So we blacks decided to build our own club. . . . You see, the club was the only offering black Cubans had." (Juan Mallea, 1987)

"When the white Cubans started getting Americanized, they became more like white Americans in their attitudes toward blacks, including black Cubans. And that extended to discrimination from all sides—from white Cubans and white Americans and also from black Americans who didn't really understand us. You can't comprehend how painful that can be." (Sylvia Griñán, 1977)

The directors of La Unión Martí-Maceo in 1917. Seated (left to right): José C. Rivas, Jacinto San Martín, Francisco Flores (president), Julio Pozo, Juan Franco. Standing (left to right): Eladio Valdés, Emilio Carcanal, Rogelio Pérez, Alejandro Hernández, Gustavo Linares, Pablo Valdés, and Juan Casellas.

"In order to keep our heritage, we organized a school at night to teach the Spanish language and Cuban history." (Francisco Rodríguez, 1987)

The first clubhouse of L'Unione Italiana (the Italian Club), a mutual aid society organized in Ybor City in 1894, was located on Seventh Avenue and dedicated in 1912. It burned down in 1916.

"The Italian Club in Ybor City is one of the largest and most flourishing of the Italian organizations. It is similar to the Spanish clubs in offering social and recreational advantages and medical services to its members. This club gives many dances and other social functions which are attended by the entire families of its membership." (Federal Writers' Project, 1937)

"My father belonged to L'Unione. Before he ever bought a loaf of bread, he paid his dues. We grew up appreciating that fact." (Domenico Giunta, 1987)

"Next to my family, L'Unione is my family." (Paul Longo, 1987)

The current Italian Club, which stands on the corner of Seventh Avenue and Eighteenth Street, was dedicated in 1918 and is shown here in 1921.

"Oh, when that was going up we were all so excited, so thrilled. Most everybody that didn't work would go out there and stand around and watch the building going up. It was a beautiful affair, a beautiful club." (Mary Pitisci Italiano, 1987)

"The present clubhouse, a substantial building in the Italian Renaissance style . . . has a theater, ballroom, library, canteen, and recreation rooms." (Federal Writers' Project, 1937)

"[The Italian Club] was the place where the men would meet to discuss their politics—topics of the day—national and local and/or the cigar makers' strikes—discussions galore, many of which took the form of debates. The place was ideal—outdoors, on the steps and on the landing leading into the club house which became a platform for the speakers. It was all spontaneous, nothing planned, but it is certain that many men went home at night looking forward to the next day to continue the debate or start a new one. These discussions always took place at dusk—after an early supper perhaps and terminated after dark." (James Mortellaro, 1987)

"I remember when the Italian Club was built. It was a nice club. . . . We [Spanish kids] used to go to dances there quite a lot as young boys, the Italian Club, also the Centro Español, Centro Asturiano, and the Cuban Club. It was a perfect setup for a young boy, because you could go there and didn't have to take a date. . . . You could always find some girls that were chaperoned." (Al López, 1987)

The game room of the Italian Club (c. 1922).

"Since the turn of the century, and even before, there was regular theater [in Ybor City]. Resident and traveling companies from Spain and Cuba would always stop off here on their way to New York. Sometimes those companies would charge $3 and $5 a ticket, which was outrageous in those times. But the people believed in their entertainment, and they didn't let a little thing like a day's pay stand in the way." (René González, 1977)

"These social clubs all had libraries, auditoriums, gyms, dance halls and canteens, where the men gathered in the evenings. At the Centro Asturiano we saw *zarzuelas* [musical comedies] performed by local amateurs. When great international performers, like Enrico Caruso, came to Tampa, it was the cigar makers who booked them, not the *americanos* on the other side of Nebraska Avenue. Saturday nights young people (properly chaperoned) went from one dance to another at the four social clubs." (Jose Yglesias, 1977)

Manuel Aparicio and Matilde de Rueda performing a play at the Centro Español during the 1930s.

The Ladies Auxiliary (1941) of the Centro Español, like women's organizations in Tampa's other mutual aid societies, engaged in a number of critical activities, especially fund-raising. Front row (left to right): Dalia González, Manuela Fernández, Socorro Alvarez, Katie Scaglione, Lolita Lado, Elvira Paniello, Josefina Pizzo, Cecilia Vázquez, Patricia Paula, Jennie Rodríguez, and Billie Douglas. Back row (left to right): Angelita Alvarez, Margarita Fernández, Benigna Fernández, Hilda Díaz, Mayita Limia, Amelia González, Paquita Escalante, Hilda Roy, Alicia Fernández, Jennie Rodiero, and Zoraida Lavandera. (Courtesy of La Gaceta)

Special edition of the Tampa Morning Tribune, March 1, 1908.

"The fire was first discovered in a room in a boarding house conducted by Antonio Díaz at Twelfth Avenue and Twentieth Street. When first seen, the flames were breaking from the windows in the second story and spread so rapidly through the frame structure that long before the fire department arrived the entire building was one mass of flames. . . . From Twelfth Avenue and Twentieth Street the fire spread to Sixteenth Street and thence to Michigan Avenue [Columbus Drive], where it finally exhausted itself." (*Tampa Morning Tribune*, March 1, 1908)

"Tampa has suffered the severest blow in all its history. The conflagration which on Sunday morning swept over Ybor City, a hurricane of flame, left desolation in its path—a desolate waste of territory, desolate families in want of bread and, worst of all, desolate hearts that ache in the intensity of their anguish." (*Tampa Morning Tribune*, March 3, 1908)

"While Fire Chief Tucker Savage attributes the spread of the Ybor City fire directly to the scarcity of water and the lack of pressure, he also asserts that the construction of buildings, and their arrangement without regard for fire protection, had much to do with the disaster." (*Tampa Morning Tribune*, March 15, 1908)

Firefighters arriving at the 1908 fire in Ybor City.

The destruction left by the 1908 fire in Ybor City.

"Over a million dollars' worth of property was destroyed, two thousand people were made homeless, a thousand expert cigar makers were thrown out of employment and the commercial life of Tampa received a serious blow yesterday morning when fire swept eighteen blocks of the most thickly populated district of Ybor City." (*Tampa Morning Tribune,* March 1, 1908)

"An investigation yesterday afternoon failed to confirm the report of a loss of human life. . . . The disastrous conflagration which visited a densely populated section of Ybor City Sunday morning . . . raged for four hours, destroying five cigar factories, fifteen restaurants, six saloons, fifteen boarding houses, twenty stores and 240 homes." (*Tampa Morning Tribune,* March 3, 1908)

A Seventh Avenue trolley (1910) that went "Direct to De Soto Park," a favorite site for Sunday picnics in Palmetto Beach, located south of Ybor City.

"There are certain characteristics which are possessed in common by the Spaniards, Italians, and Cubans. . . . Sunday is usually given over to picnics and other forms of recreation. The Spanish gather at their casinos and sanatoriums; the Cubans and Italians, with families, in the various parks belonging to the trolley systems." (U.S. Immigration Commission, 1911)

An outing by members of the Centro Español in honor of the Spanish ambassador (1911).

"Several hundred members of El Centro Español together with members of other Spanish societies held an enjoyable picnic at Palmetto Beach yesterday, the purpose being to raise the sum of $800 which is needed to paint the interior of the sanatorium on Bayshore Boulevard. An admission fee was charged as is usual, and it is likely that the fund will be raised. One of the features of the day that drew special attention and greatly pleased both young and old was the presence of Señor Ramón García Libardón, one of the old-time Spanish pipers, who played several times during the day to large and greatly interested audiences. Señor Libardón is a native of the province of Asturias." (*Tampa Daily Times,* April 27, 1914)

"It was a different world. Everyone spoke Italian or Spanish, and they were all oriented to their clubs. The club was the 'mecca.' . . . There was so much going on—the whole social focus was on the clubs. Some of the activities in the summertime were picnics, and they were very enjoyable. Rocky Point, Ballast Point, and De Soto Park in Palmetto Beach were very popular sites. . . . When one of the clubs gave a picnic, people of different nationalities attended." (Tony Pizzo, 1980)

Members of the Italian Club, gathering at the corner of Seventh Avenue and Eighteenth Street to form a caravan for a picnic trip (c. 1912). The present Italian Club stands on the empty lot to the right.

Members of Círculo Cubano attending a picnic at Rocky Point during the 1920s.

"There were a lot of picnics in those days, too. Different clubs and societies of Ybor City like the Centro Asturiano, Centro Español, Centro Italiano, would sell picnics. . . . Some of the wealthier men would buy many tickets, then give them away to kids and friends so there were always a lot of people, see, and a lot of noise and everybody bringing the cauldrons full of food." (Virgilio Valdez, 1973)

"Ballast Point Park is located on the west shore of Hillsborough Bay, about four miles southwest of the city. This popular picnic and amusement park contains some sixteen acres of rich tropical foliage, lawns, etc., in a high state of cultivation. Salt water bathing is one of the main attractions, the beach being equipped with a large bathing house, where suits may be rented. Boats and fishing tackle may be rented at the dock for fishing trips off the point. Shore dinners are served in the café. The open-air dancing pavilion and theater is one of the best in the state, and dancing is a regular attraction throughout the year." (*Rinaldi's Guide Book to the City of Tampa, 1915–16 Edition*, 1915)

"When the trolley line . . . was finished . . . you could then transfer to the trolleys that ran the length of Bayshore Boulevard to Ballast Point on the farthest tip of Tampa Bay. . . . Each family brought baskets of food and sat under the trees or fished at the pier or danced at the pavilion." (Jose Yglesias, 1971)

The pavilion at Ballast Point.

La Unión Martí-Maceo sponsored El Club Juvenil, whose members dressed in the traditional attire of country people in Cuba (1934).

"We had a full calendar of community events at La Unión Martí-Maceo, our own black Cuban community center: Frequent Latin dances, traveling vaudeville shows from Cuba, and an occasional play in Spanish that we staged ourselves rounded out a busy schedule for our community." (Evelio Grillo, 2000)

"Latin cigar workers organized the first baseball club in Ybor City about 1887. The Cuban and El Porvenir clubs soon followed and baseball became a popular sport." (Federal Writers' Project, 1937)

"The Tampa and Ybor City baseball clubs played a game in Ybor City last Sunday evening, and [los] Cubanos walloped the Tampas badly." (*Tampa Tribune*, September 27, 1888)

"We didn't have radio, TV, nothing like that; we just had to play baseball. . . . Sometimes everybody would chip in a nickel or a dime or whatever they could to buy one ball, and that's what we had—one ball, or else we'd put black tape around it after we'd hit for quite a while and play with that. We used to have to build our own diamonds. Any sandlot that we could, we'd put a diamond there and we'd play in the neighborhood some place. . . . They were mostly Latin kids." (Al López, 1985)

"The boys in the neighborhood had a half-block of land on which to play baseball, about which the entire town was passionate. The larger and bigger boys, dreaming of major-league careers, played the game seriously and well enough to attract large crowds of older men returning from work. These men took up collections to keep the teams supplied with balls, bats, gloves, and other equipment." (Evelio Grillo, 2000)

An Ybor City baseball team.

"I started to play baseball on the Armendariz team in 1908. In those days you had to play every position. My last ten years on the team I was pitcher." (Manuel Santos, 1968)

"We are having some good ball games in this neck of the woods, and many of the cigar makers . . . show big team stuff. Pitcher Fernández is holding a fine record against teams like Lakeland, Orlando, Sanford and Bartow." (*United States Tobacco Journal*, August 23, 1919)

The baseball team of the Cuesta-Rey cigar factory, including A. L. Cuesta, Jr. (far left), won the Cigar City League championship in 1913. (Courtesy of Nonita Cuesta-Henson)

A baseball game at West Tampa's Macfarlane Park in 1922. (Courtesy of Tampa–Hillsborough County Public Library System)

"I was with the [Tampa] 'Smokers.' . . . Oh, we'd draw. You'd be surprised. . . . At that time the cigar makers were on what they call piece time. Whatever they made, that's what they earned. The games started at 3:15, so by 2:30 they would leave the factory and come out and see the ball game. . . . And the people, the cigar makers, were great. I think that was our greatest draw." (Al López, 1985)

"Cigar manufacturers generally breathe a sigh of relief at the close of the local baseball season which, throughout its duration, kept a large number of cigar makers away from their benches for two or more afternoons each week. Most of the players were cigar makers and their friends and admirers followed them to the games, thus losing the entire afternoon's work." (*Tobacco Leaf,* October 16, 1913)

"During the World Series the local Spanish-language daily newspaper provided an elaborate mechanical display which represented the action from wherever the games were being played. Shiny metal balls represented the players, and the game could be followed as the balls moved around a magnetic board. It seemed that the entirety of Ybor City gathered in front of the mesmerizing display, cheering or booing depending upon the course of the game." (Evelio Grillo, 2000)

"The World Series worked havoc with production here . . . resulting from the progress of masses of workers from the factories Wednesday when hundreds left at two o'clock for the big electric boards of the two local papers, giving rise to rumors of a walkout. They were all back early the next morning [and] but only for quick action by the manufacturers would have repeated the next day. Cuesta, Rey & Co. got busy and installed a radiophone with an amplifier which gave the games play-by-play to their big force and practically every factory in Tampa got the score by half innings and called it to the workers." (*Tobacco Leaf,* October 14, 1922)

Ybor City residents listening to a World Series game broadcast in Spanish by the local newspaper La Traducción *during the 1930s.*

A boxing ring set up behind the Cuban Club during the 1920s. (Courtesy of Florida State Archives)

"The Cuban . . . is a great lover of sports, especially baseball, boxing, and cockfighting. He loves to gamble on practically anything that contains an element of chance. . . . The athletic division [of the Cuban Club] began to give exhibitions of amateur boxing. . . . After the arena was built, the crowd increased and the arena had to be enlarged." (Federal Writers' Project, 1937)

The women's basketball team of the Corral-Wodiska cigar factory, posing after winning a title in 1930. Their uniforms carried the name "Bering," the company's leading brand. Standing (left to right): Magdalena Navarro, Elvira Vásquez, Mary López, Caroline Giovenco, the team manager (name unknown), Oliva Alvarez, Josephine García, Frances Campisi, and Lily Durán. Sitting are Guillermina García and Mary Penzato. (Courtesy of La Gaceta)

"West Tampa was just like the wild west—a frontier town. There were cockfights, boxing matches, wrestling matches, horses tied to hitching posts in front of cantinas, gambling and loud arguments about politics in America, Cuba and Spain. But it was not bad. It was in the spirit of fun and it was a way of relaxation after long hours of making cigars." (Alfredo Prende, 1977)

Main Street in West Tampa (c. 1911) at the corner of Howard Avenue. (Courtesy of Tampa–Hillsborough County Public Library System)

"Cockfighting is generally the order of the day on Sundays at Ybor City. A Cuban generally turns to such things to pass the time, and time spent trying to civilize them is wasted." (*Tampa Tribune*, March 8, 1888)

"Some of the residents of this city especially among the Cuban population seem to have very little decency in their composition. You can at any time of the day if you promenade along the streets of Ybor City or West Tampa see children from the ages of one to several years playing around in the garb which nature gave them with a little additional covering of dirt or cheese-cloth, generally the former, while the smiling parents watch them without a word of reproof." (*Tampa Morning Tribune*, August 4, 1896)

West Tampa residents preparing for a cockfight in 1915. (Courtesy of Arsenio Sánchez)

An Ybor City saloon at the corner of Twelfth Avenue and Eighteenth Street in 1900.

"After receiving their weekly pay on Saturdays, it is customary [for cigar workers] to pay their board bills, and then start in to gamble away the remainder. They only stop when they either have lost all their money or won from all comers. . . . And then, they go back to work, which is usually on Tuesday morning of each week. Scarcely any factory works Monday with anything like half their force, owing to the prevailing gambling spirit among the men." (*United States Tobacco Journal*, July 25, 1896

"An enterprising Spaniard, Manuel Suárez, better known as *El Gallego* (the Galician) . . . moved to Ybor City and introduced bolita to Tampa. . . . In the early 1890s *El Gallego* opened a saloon in the Sevilla Building on the northeast corner of Fourteenth Street and Eighth Avenue. Here he introduced the friendly, sociable game of chance known as bolita, or 'little ball.' . . . In 1927 the vicinity boasted the presence of approximately 300 bolita joints. More than 1,200 bolita peddlers made the rounds of the city, covering cigar factories, homes, office and government buildings. Almost everyone in Tampa played bolita. The nickel and dime game established by *El Gallego* had become a social monster—a multi-million dollar dragon." (Tony Pizzo, 1983)

"Bolita (little ball) is the most popular gambling game among Cubans. . . . Tickets are sold at the bolita house and by agents who go from door to door. The players buy tickets bearing the number they hope will win. The tickets cost five cents each, and each winning ticket pays the holder $4. At the bolita 'throwing' a group of interested persons (players, spectators) gather in the bolita house. A tray, holding 100 small balls consecutively numbered, is displayed for examination by the group. The balls are then placed in a bag, which is passed around and thoroughly shaken; finally it is tossed by the bolita operator into the group of spectators, one of whom catches it by one of the balls inside. Closely watched, the operator proceeds to cut the bag, releasing the ball held by the spectator. The number on that ball is the winning number." (Federal Writers' Project, 1935)

"Sometimes, the people running a bolita racket would size up the day's receipts and see that very few people had bet on, say, ball number eleven. What they do is pull that ball out of the bag, put it on a block of ice for a few minutes, then put it back in. When it came time to toss the bag for the lottery, they'd throw it to an inside man, who appeared to the crowd to be just another guy, and he'd feel around in the bag until he located the cold ball. Then he'd move that ball to the bottom of the bag very carefully, so no one would see, isolate it from the rest, just like always, and take a knife and slice it off. Number eleven wins." (Charles Otero, 1977)

Bolita balls, including one with a lead center to cheat gamblers by making it possible for "an inside man" to distinguish the weighted ball from the lighter ones.

El Dorado, a gambling house at the corner of Eighth Avenue and Fourteenth Street, also served alcohol during Prohibition.

"[Cigar makers] loved to bet. At that time [in the 1920s] gambling in Tampa was wide open. They had gambling houses; you could go in there, and they had roulette, dice, everything, just wide open. It was during Prohibition; you could go to any of those Spanish restaurants. You'd want a bottle, I mean, a drink of Canadian Club. They'd put the bottle of Canadian Club, you'd help yourself. A bottle of German beer, a dollar for a bottle of beer, right on the counter. It was wide open." (Al López, 1985)

"Bolita and other forms of gambling in and around Tampa are controlled by an Ybor City group. . . . Charlie Wall [was] boss gambler in Tampa. . . . Most of Wall's associates then were Tampans of Spanish or Cuban ancestry. Few were Italians, although the Italians and Sicilians always wanted to get in on the Tampa bolita bank. It was natural, therefore, for the Italian groups to consolidate, with the result that today all members of the syndicate but one are Italian." (*Tampa Morning Tribune*, October 6, 1947)

Ybor City's Seventh Avenue (1923), facing east from Fourteenth Street, with Café El Central on the left.

"Ybor City is like stepping from one country into another. . . . It is a revelation to many to pass through the atmosphere in that section, truly Latin, with habits and customs almost identical with those of Cuba. The main business district of Ybor City is stretched along Seventh Avenue, lined on either side with a white way, supported by the merchants, equal to anything in Tampa. . . . The streets of Ybor City are usually lined with people from five o'clock in the afternoon until late at night. The restaurants are always open as well as many of the stores. Saturday night, Seventh Avenue is literally lined with them—they have just received their week's pay and are shopping for Sunday and the following week." (*Tampa Daily Times*, February 17, 1917)

"With their Latin clubs, Spanish restaurants, coffee houses, Spanish newspapers, theaters and numerous social functions, the Spanish and Cuban workmen are as much at home in this city as they are in Cuba." (*Tampa Daily Times*, July 26, 1924)

"Approximately 6,000 persons attended dances held at four Latin clubs of Ybor City and West Tampa Saturday night and Sunday. . . . The dance at the Cuban Club held Saturday night was the annual carnival dance of the recreation committee and was attended by 2,500 persons. American music was furnished in the main ballroom of the club and Cuban music in the second floor of the club house. The dance halls were elaborately decorated." (*Tampa Daily Times*, March 10, 1930)

"The Centro Español became the center of our social life. This was the most important place every Sunday for all of us to come and gather. . . . I had to come with my aunt and my cousin and my sister, and we would all troop here and my aunt would sit in a corner and we would dance and have a good time." (Maria Passetti, 1988)

A dance at the Centro Asturiano (1931).

"Seventh Avenue was a vibrant main drag; it probably surpassed Franklin Street at one time. The best shops in Tampa were on Seventh Avenue. Payday in the factories was on Saturday, so you can imagine thousands of cigar makers getting their pay, going home and taking a bath, putting on their best finery, and walking down Seventh Avenue. The shops stayed open on Saturday until eleven. That's the reason Saturday night dances in the Latin clubs started after the shops closed at eleven." (Tony Pizzo, 1980)

"The cigar factory workers are people of distinctive habits. . . . It is said that no class of workers are more liberal in the expenditure of their wages than are the cigar factory employees. . . . They are cash and carry shoppers, never disdaining the armful of bundles collected on the shopping tour, and going through the crush of a crowd smiling and patient." (*Tampa Daily Times*, December 20, 1922)

Seventh Avenue in 1926. (Courtesy of Tampa–Hillsborough County Public Library System)

Tampa cigar makers (c. 1920), including the father (second from right) of the writer Jose Yglesias. (Courtesy of Dalia Corro)

"It was a Latin town. Men didn't sit at home. They went to the cafés, on street corners, at the Labor Temple, which they built themselves." (Jose Yglesias, 1970)

"We always had money; we weren't broke. If you made 250 cigars a day, you were good—you had to be fast to make 200. I used to make 300 a day. It was a good trade for a fast man." (Armando Valdés, Sr., 1969)

An Ybor City café.

"Up the street a short way, a coffee house is encountered. About small tables will be found men, and sometimes women, fraternizing over the much-talked-of Cuban coffee and vari-colored pastries. A waiter approaches with a huge pot in either hand. Into a glass mug he pours a quantity of hot milk and on top of it he adds a dash of thick black coffee—that's Cuban coffee." (*Tampa Daily Times,* October 23, 1924)

"Ours was a cigar-making community that kept U.S. working hours, and although on ordinary days the men went after dinner to the canteens at the Cuban, Spanish, Asturian, and Italian clubs to play dominoes and chat and have a second cup of *café solo* with perhaps a *trago* of cognac, everyone was back home and ready for bed at eleven o'clock." (Jose Yglesias, 1977)

"Step from an automobile at Seventh Avenue and Fifteenth Street, and in no other place in the country could a typical Latin environment be simulated. In a way it is like taking a dream trip to Cuba. On every side the Spanish language is to be heard. Signs portray their intent in a foreign language. Quaint shops and coffee houses display wares typically destined to appeal almost exclusively to the Latin mind. Enter one of the larger Latin clubs and there will be found a scene to be found nowhere else in this country. No word of English will be heard. Characteristic games of all description, one of the principal being dominoes, are receiving enthusiastic participation from hundreds of Tampa workmen gathered there to while away an evening." (*Tampa Daily Times,* October 23, 1924)

Seventh Avenue, facing west from Fifteenth Street (1920).

Max Argintar's store on Seventh Avenue included a pawnshop.

"I remember the stores along Seventh Avenue and how Jewish merchants, mostly from Romania, mingled so well with other merchants and were so much a part of the business community. These Jewish merchants included Steinberg's, Segal's shoe store, Verkauf's 'The Rainbow,' Little Katz (called *El Gatito* by the Latin community), and Max Argintar, whose fine store is still at the same location." (Braulio Alonso, 1997)

"My father [Max Argintar] was born in Beserabia, Romania. . . . [When] he opened up a store, he had luggage, jewelry and it became a pawnshop [with] guns and what have you. . . .. My father . . . could speak Romanian, he could speak Yiddish, he knew Hebrew, he knew English, he knew Spanish and he knew Italian and some Greek. And the customers were Italians [and] Spaniards. . . . All the Jewish merchants on the Avenue spoke Spanish and Italian." (Sammy Argintar, 2000)

"It was a position of importance to make the cigar. It was the lifeblood of the community. And pride in yourself and your craft demanded you to put total concentration and effort into the job. At the end of the day you go home tired, but you would talk with the family, have dinner, relax and play with the young ones and you were fresh again. Then, maybe you would go to town." (Honorato Henry Domínguez, 1997)

"The records of a large number of factories show that their production on Monday of every week is just about fifty percent of the average daily production, and that Saturday figures are about the same. Therefore, it is reasonable to presume that only half a day is actually put on by the operators on those two days." (*Tobacco Leaf,* November 30, 1916)

Seventh Avenue (1927) with the Centro Español (center right).

"I remember Seventh Avenue as a central attraction on Saturday nights. Girls, accompanied by other girls or relatives, would stroll in one direction along the avenue and young men would stroll in the opposite direction on the same sidewalk. These continuous concentric circles offered an opportunity for young men and women to meet and flirt." (Braulio Alonso, 1997)

"Saturday was a big day in Ybor City. All the young people went to La Séptima (Seventh Avenue) to see if we could find a special person. Boys and girls would crowd Seventh Avenue, trying to attract attention without being obvious. We would walk from Fourteenth Street to Eighteenth or Twenty-first on one side, then cross to the other side. This promenade would last from early evening until 10:30 p.m. . . . Then everyone would go home. Few of the boys and girls would hold hands, as that would have implied a commitment." (Ramón Moré, 1990)

"Mother would take us walking up and down Seventh Avenue, and all the boys would be standing on the curb and the mothers would look like little hens watching their chicks. So that nobody would touch us." (Angelina Spoto Comescone, 1987)

A Saturday night on Seventh Avenue (1929).

Las Novedades restaurant in 1929.

"Each nationality has imported its native cuisine. Perhaps the *cocinero* will defile his art for gold and prepare steaks American style, but he would rather concoct the famed *arroz con pollo* (chicken and rice), yellow with saffron, and the black bean soup, or the *garbanzo sopa* (Spanish bean soup). These delectable dishes are served with gracious smiles, string music, and often with floor shows. For those who lack funds or capacity to enjoy elaborate dinners, the Cuban sandwich, at a dime, is equal to a five-course meal. Blanketed between chunks of hard-crusted bread cut from a long loaf is a generous portion of seasoned meats." (Federal Writers' Project, 1941)

"The early Ybor City Latin restaurant workers were a strange lot, as well as being a very hard-working group. Those who joined the ranks were quickly given an alias. It was Benny Fernández (alias Benny Lucas) who baptized my dad José Abad '*Submarino*' at Las Novedades. It was witnessed by José Coto (*Filete Sin Hueso*) and handsome Louis Pérez (*Bicicleta*). When I started working at Las Novedades in 1947, Benny promptly named me *Torpedo Numero Cuatro*." (Joseph M. Abad, 1997)

"When the Latins arrived in Florida, educational facilities were extremely limited. The Latin clubs therefore established schools of their own, where reading, writing, arithmetic, commercial subjects, and music were taught in Spanish." (Stetson Kennedy, 1942)

"Older members of the Latin elements are content to live unto themselves. . . . Thousands of them who spent their lives in Ybor City are unable to speak or read the English language. With their own social life; their own business establishments where Spanish and Italian are spoken almost exclusively and catering to Latin needs; their own theaters, churches, clubs, restaurants and saloons where English is seldom heard; with newspapers in their own language, and most of them being employed in cigar factories conducted by their own nationals, the majority of residents feel little need or desire for American contacts." (Federal Writers' Project, 1937)

"I remember that the *lingua franca* was Spanish and that Italian/Sicilian was spoken almost everywhere in the community. It gave us the opportunity to learn each other's language." (Braulio Alonso, 1997)

Ybor City children in the 1890s at the Liceo Cubano, where they learned to read and write Spanish.

Students at the West Tampa Methodist Church School (1924). (Courtesy of Tampa–Hillsborough County Public Library System)

"Ybor City is certainly a broad field for mission work. With a population of 10,000, the majority of whom are utterly indifferent to the gospel of Jesus Christ, our little band of workers seems courageous indeed to contend against so much ignorance and superstition. The conditions in Ybor City are peculiar. Among the men there is a great deal of atheism." (Women's Home Mission Society, 1904)

"The moving population of Cubans, Spaniards, Italians, and Sicilians never comes to Church (not three percent of them); most of them have no respect for religion or priest and many will not have their children baptized and many are married outside the Church." (Rev. William J. Tyrell, 1911)

"The male Latin here, whether Spanish, Italian or Cuban, will go Sunday morning and most every evening to their respective clubs. . . . During the weekdays, because he works in the factory, his night recreation is the clubs, Sunday from morning until night in his club again, thereby leaving the Church and its services out of his mode of living." (Federal Writers' Project, 1935)

Students at West Tampa's Drew School (1917), which was located on the corner of Armenia Avenue and Cordilia Street. (Courtesy of Arsenio Sánchez)

"I was born [in 1919] and raised in Tampa, or rather, in a section of the city called Ybor City, where only Spanish was spoken. My father, a peasant from Galicia, immigrated to Havana as an adolescent to work as an apprentice in a cigar factory. When he became a cigar maker, he moved to Tampa to search for work in the cigar factories of Ybor City. Ybor City was a Latin island in the South of the United States, and I did not speak a word of English when I entered public school. There, we students spoke Spanish among ourselves and broken English with the teachers." (Jose Yglesias, 1991)

"I remember the day when I first realized I was thinking in English. I was thirteen and a half, and I was looking at a sketch of the Parthenon in our junior-high-school library." (Jose Yglesias, 1963)

"I remember the various types of housing. There were the '*cañones*' or cannon houses. These houses had a long hall with rooms along the hall. One could fire a cannon down the hall and hit nothing, hence the name. . . . Lots were small, and the houses close together. Houses were of wood. There was no air conditioning, and windows were kept open during warm weather." (Braulio Alonso, 1997)

"The houses on our block, all identical, stood very close to one another, about four feet apart. They were either unpainted or had not been painted in years. They sat on brick pilings, about four feet off the ground. The roof, built of corrugated tin sheets, had no insulation between it and the ceilings of the rooms below it. A strong rain made a great noise, sheer excitement for me. . . . We bathed in a large tin tub set in the middle of the kitchen, the water heated in buckets on the stove. The rooms were heated with kerosene stoves. . . . We must have been very poor at that time, but I don't remember *feeling* poor." (Evelio Grillo, 2000)

"In my time we didn't have radio; we didn't have a television. So we sat on the porch and socialized with out next-door neighbors." (Josephine Castellano, 1988)

A typical Ybor City home (c. 1930).

Ybor City homes on Twelfth Avenue (c. 1930).

"The old-time Latin family was an economic unit, in which all the members worked and contributed to the financial and social well-being of the family. Young ones would get married and move back in—start having babies—while the older ones lived out their last days under the same roof and those of middle age kept on plugging. It was common for one family to maintain a single house generation after generation with it absolutely necessary to use the Spanish language." (Oscar Aguayo, 1977)

"There's a lot of value in growing up with older people in the house. It teaches you a lot of things you would never get elsewhere. It prepares you to deal with most any situation that comes up because most any story an elderly Latin person tells has a lesson or moral in it. It gives you character." (Aída Alvarez, 1977)

"The ties of family are the strongest there are." (Jose Yglesias, 1963)

"In the home life the cigar workers are indeed faithful providers, and show remarkable tenderness in their family relations. Nearly all the families boast of several children, and their love of children is remarkable. In fact, the very liberality accorded their children ofttimes leads one to think there is no restraint placed upon the young boy or girl. This is not the case, however, as great stress is placed upon parental respect and morals that lead to better manhood or womanhood. While the occupation of parents, which in many cases takes both mother and father to the factory, leaves the children to themselves, or the guidance of others, the youngsters, with very few exceptions, progress through the various juvenile stages with a success that is very commendable. Many follow in the steps of their parents and are found 'learning the trade' when their school term is brought to a close." (*Tampa Daily Times*, December 20, 1922)

The children of Ybor City cigar maker Carlos Manrique (c. 1906): (left to right) Wilfredo, Dahlia, and Charles. (Courtesy of Art Maynor)

Jose Yglesias (right) and his cousin Nora
Fernández (c. 1925) were both the children
of Ybor City cigar workers. (Courtesy of
Dalia Corro)

An Ybor City youngster dressed
as a rumba dancer (c. 1930).

"Games were made by us in Ybor City. Our parents approved of these games 100 percent, as all the equipment required zero cash. . . . *El palito* was composed of any old corn broom handle that was sawed off into two sections. The *palito* was about six inches long, and one end was sharpened to a point. When it was laid down on the old red bricks that paved our Ybor streets and hit by our 'bats' (the other section of the corn broom handle, usually about two feet long), it would jump into the air. The object was to hit the *palito* while in the air, and a good hit would really make it fly. The 'batter' would stand inside a ring that was drawn on the red bricks about five to six feet in diameter. The 'outfielders' would try to catch the *palito* on the fly. If they did, it was an 'out.' If the *palito* hit the ground, the fielders would throw the *palito* towards the ring, hoping that it fell inside the ring or on the line. This was also an out. The sides would change after three outs, batters to the outfield and fielders to bat." (Emilio A. Rodríguez, 1997)

Sammy and Peter Giglio in the delivery truck of their father, Lorenzo, who ran a West Tampa store. (Courtesy of Rose Giglio)

Children on Ybor City's Fifth Avenue playing on fallen power poles after the 1921 hurricane.

Ybor City's "Piruli Man."

"'The Piruli Man,' Luis Pérez . . . was small in stature, about five feet three inches, a native of Cuba. He had black, wavy hair, the characteristic Latin look. . . . He was a vendor in Ybor City, selling a hard candy made in a cone shape, similar in taste to rock candy. Though he used many different colors, red, yellow, blue, etc., the flavor was basically the same. He took a banana stalk discarded from a produce market. This stalk proved to be very convenient for transporting his *pirulis.* Since each candy had a stick (sharp like a toothpick) for a handle, this enabled him to stick them into the banana stalk and display them for sale. . . . He had a favorite whistle—very original— which set him apart from the other vendors. His slogan was '*Con dinero o sin dinero,*' meaning with money or without money. With money, you could buy a *piruli* for a penny. Without money, you could purchase a *piruli* with three redeemable coupons, which appeared on Octagon Soap, Clabber Girl baking powder, and Golden Key evaporated milk." (Gus Rodríguez, 1997)

An Italian wedding in Ybor City (1928).

"In my generation in high school, if we dated a Latin girl, we had to have a chaperone. The mother would usually go along. Dating started at high school age. So we had to take the mothers to the movies with us, or to dances." (Tony Pizzo, 1980)

"If you even sat on the porch outside . . . somebody had to be there." (Mary Pitisci Italiano, 1987)

"Marriage was the only way, the only way to get from out, from under the skirts of the mother. . . . We thought that by getting married young—you see we couldn't see a fella, couldn't sit on the porch with the light on at night—so the first [man] to come along and smile at us, we would marry him. *And* there was not divorce." (Rosemary Scaglione Craparo, 1987)

"My parents met in Key West. My father was born in Tampa. His father died when he was two years old and then my grandmother moved back to Key West. My mother was born in Key West, and back in the twenties my father began courting her. They married in 1929 and came to Ybor City, where they worked in the cigar factories. My father was a union man—a selector (*rezagadore*). My mother worked too, but she stayed home when she started having children. She had four children. . . . My father was more Cuban than José Martí himself. He was a hellava patriot. The radio in our house was tuned to Cuba. Pure static, but my father would say, 'Don't change that station.' My mother was second generation, but she spoke very, very little English." (Al Sánchez, 2001)

Clemencia and Alfredo Sánchez, both cigar workers, on their wedding day in 1929. (Courtesy of Al Sánchez)

The Ybor City Italian Brass Band (1916), conducted by Giovanni Mazarelli (far right), played at weddings, funerals, and festivals.

"One of the most peculiar, yet impressive sights the *Tribune* has observed for many days, was an Italian funeral in Ybor City Saturday. The customary rule of the corpse riding in the hearse is entirely done away with, although the hearse occupied a prominent position in the procession. The corpse is carried by four large men with uplifted hats, followed by a brass band, then an empty hearse and carriage precede the regular concourse of sorrowing relatives and sobbing friends. The empty vehicles designate that the home is vacant. The funeral was conducted in a very solemn and impressive manner, although a little peculiar to the general run of Americans." (*Tampa Morning Tribune* [Weekly Edition], October 13, 1893)

An Italian funeral procession in Ybor City (1901), showing the original building of Our Lady of Mercy Catholic Church.

"A unique form of expression of grief and sympathy developed in Ybor City. At first, the deceased was kept at home, usually in the living room in an open coffin for several days. The house was open for visitors all day and most of the night. Everyone brought over flowers, food, or some memento or memorabilia involving the deceased. Later, after funeral homes took over the wake function, turnout for the wake function was large with hundreds of mourners paying their respect. An interesting aspect of these wakes was that wakes became a social gathering as well as a popular place for politicians to be seen." (Víctor J. Martínez, 1997)

The Boza funeral home in West Tampa.

The Centro Asturiano cemetery.

"The old custom of long and ostentatious mourning for deceased relatives among the Cuban and Spanish has been somewhat changed in recent years. The old custom required the widow to wear solid black for at least a year after the death of her husband, while the widower wore a black band around his arm and a black tie for a like period. The mourning is longer in many cases, and today may be seen women in Ybor City who are wearing black twenty or thirty years after the death of a loved one. During the mourning period no one in the family is supposed to take part in any festival or other public amusement." (Federal Writers' Project, 1937)

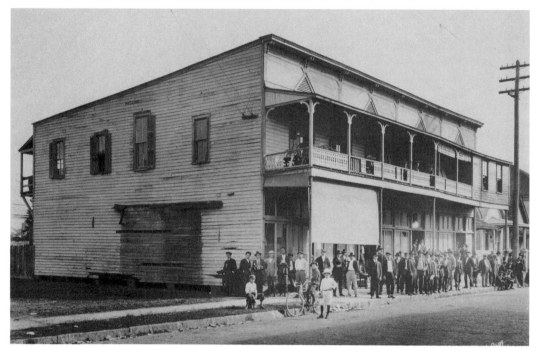

Workers gathered during 1919 in front of Ybor City's Labor Temple, where cigar workers had their union offices.

"The Latin cigar maker considers himself more of an artist than a worker. This feeling has caused him to resent plant rules and restrictions and oppose measures which are a part of the standard discipline in American plants. . . . He has a tendency to take things pertaining to his work or his art, as he thinks of it, very seriously. . . . Once an issue is before him, he will fight desperately for it, which helps explain some of the controversies between the workers and employers in the industry. Many of the employers, for their part, are just as stubborn about compromising an issue." (A. Stuart Campbell, 1939)

"We are going to try to make Tampa 100 percent union, for the cigar makers that are working here in Tampa see by this time that they cannot stand alone. If they ask for anything, it is always the Cigar Makers' International Union that they have to look in order to receive anything. . . . At the present time we have a few shops 100 percent organized." (*Cigar Makers' Official Journal*, December 1919)

A cartoon from Tobacco Leaf, August 5, 1920.

"When I was little, they had a strike in 1920. It lasted [ten] months. It was for the same old thing. They said, 'You ask too much.' It was hard, I tell you." (Dolores Río, 1987)

"The cigar makers of Tampa are fighting for an American right, 'collective bargaining.'" (Local 474, Cigar Makers' International Union, August 1920)

"By refusing to recognize the [Cigar Makers' International Union], the manufacturers and their loyal workers have truly saved the industry. They have saved it from radical control." (Tampa Cigar Manufacturers' Association, November 1920)

A mass meeting of striking cigar workers, held on October 14, 1920, at the Centro Asturiano, during the ten months' strike by 12,000 workers who unsuccessfully sought union recognition and the union shop.

"During the 1920 strike I went to Cuba to work. The union here paid my way to Cuba and back. I was in Cuba about a year. I tell you one thing, in those days I didn't leave here willingly. But I would rather die than work here during the strike." (Manuel Santos, 1968)

"The manufacturers are victors in the fight to keep the industry on an open [shop] basis." (*Tampa Morning Tribune,* February 5, 1921)

"The halt is only temporary and there shall never be peace in the local cigar industry until the rights of the workers are recognized by the bosses." (*El Internacional* [Tampa], February 5, 1921)

"People date their lives from the various strikes in Tampa. When they refer to a scab, they say: 'It's no surprise he's trying to break this strike since his mother did it in 1921.' In my hometown, strikes were passionate affairs." (Jose Yglesias, 1970)

"The historians never mention the real heroes of Ybor City—the merchants who provided everything during the long and dreadful strikes that lasted as long as eleven months. When a cigar strike started, the grocers, bakers, fish markets and dairy owners kept on selling on credit to striking workers even though they knew their customers couldn't pay them. The store owners often couldn't pay their suppliers, and some went under." (Ramón Moré, 1990)

"Neighborhood grocery stores extended credit, and accounts were generally settled at the end of the week. These many grocery stores were life savers during the times workers lost their jobs temporarily and during the work stoppages and strikes that occurred during the years. The workers were without income at these times. These small grocery stores extended credit for long periods of time, or many families would have suffered severely. And workers tried to pay them back. These stores deserve the gratitude of the community." (Braulio Alonso, 1997)

The Bodega La Concha (c. 1930) on Twelfth Avenue in Ybor City.

A cartoon from Tobacco Leaf (November 24, 1921) presented the manufacturers' view of a brief strike over the removal of readers following the ten months' strike.

"4,000 West Tampa cigar workers went on strike yesterday. . . . The main point of contention was the low scale paid the workers in every branch of the various factories. Another grievance voiced was the lack of readers in the various factories. It is said the cigar makers have always paid the readers and that this feature is now absolutely banned by the majority of factories." (*Tampa Morning Tribune*, November 18, 1921)

"The Cigar Manufacturers' Association rejected all of the demands of the cigar makers. . . . The readers, it is charged, read propaganda to the men instead of matters of general interest that would make the work easier and more interesting." (*Tampa Daily Times*, November 21, 1921)

"To prolong the strike further would cause great sacrifices to the cigar makers; therefore, from the instant of this manifesto, all of the cigar makers are at liberty to return to their work." (Cigar Makers' International Union, November 29, 1921)

"By a vote of about four to one, the cigar makers of Tampa last Friday in a referendum expressed themselves in favor of a return of readers in factories. There have been no readers in the factories since the 1920 strike." (*Tobacco Leaf*, September 25, 1926)

"Men to read to cigar makers employed in Tampa factories will be engaged within the next few weeks, under arrangements being worked out between the Cigar Manufacturers' Association and employees in the factories." (*Tobacco Leaf*, September 27, 1926)

"Regulations probably will call for reading of newspapers for one hour mornings and readings of novels for three hours in the afternoons. The reading material will be passed on by a committee appointed to eliminate all racy or radical literature." (*Tampa Daily Times*, September 27, 1926)

"The advent of the readers came this week. Last week was given over by cigar makers to the selection of readers. . . . One by one favored scholars entered the busy work rooms and paraded their best styles, and one by one they won favor in this factory or that, according to the vote of their listeners." (*Tobacco Leaf*, October 16, 1926)

A lector at the Perfecto-García factory (1930), following the return of readers in 1926.

"The owners believed that because the readers read a paper like the *Daily Worker* [of the Communist Party] that they were influencing the cigar workers to make trouble. We were not responsible for the material we read. The cigar makers decided what we read." (Wilfredo Rodríguez, 1981)

"I started [working] in a cigar factory [in 1925]. . . . I learned the trade of picking and packing cigars. . . . The first Communist Party that I joined [was] in 1930. In the Labor Temple we put an office especially to organize. . . . It was the beginning of the depression. We were hungry and on relief. . . . They were throwing people out of the houses because they could not afford to pay the rent. . . . With the Communist Party, [protests] became more organized. We had marches in Ybor City. . . . As soon as we organized, we joined the Communist Party of the United States. We started working and we controlled the Labor Temple and we controlled the majority of offices of the unions. . . . Back in the Thirties we used to get the *Daily Worker*. . . . The regular newspaper was *The Worker*." (José Alvarez, 1983)

A reader at the Cuesta-Rey factory (1930).

TAMPA SUNDAY TRIBUNE

TAMPA, FLORIDA, SUNDAY, NOVEMBER 8, 1931   44 PAGES   PRICE TEN CENTS

OFFICER SHOT, OTHERS HURT IN CLASH WITH COMMUNIST MOB HERE

Police Arrest 15 After
Brief Skirmish at
Labor Temple

"A group of Tampa, Florida, workers yesterday told the *Daily Worker* of the frame-up of twenty-four Tampa workers on charges, as a result of a brutal attack upon a workers' meeting November 7, celebrating the fourteenth anniversary of the Russian Revolution." (*Daily Worker*, November 13, 1931)

"A policeman was shot, another was struck with a brick and several suffered minor injuries as officers clashed with a crowd at a communist meeting last night at the Labor Temple, Eighth Avenue near Fourteenth Street. . . . Patrolmen J. N. Byrd was seriously wounded but hopes were held for his recovery. . . . Fifteen communists were arrested. Blackjacks were swung and bricks flew freely as the communists rushed the policemen and attempted to start the parade in celebration of the fourteenth anniversary of the Soviet Union. A permit for the parade had been refused by Mayor Robert E. Lee Chancey." (*Tampa Morning Tribune*, November 8, 1931)

"The county solicitor has filed an information charging seventeen men and women with participating in an unlawful assembly, riotous conduct and assault with intent to murder the policeman." (Edwin L. Bryan, 1932)

TAMPA MORNING TRIBUNE

TAMPA, FLORIDA, FRIDAY, NOVEMBER 27, 1931 — 18 PAGES

INDUSTRY HERE STOPS CIGAR PLANT READING

Takes Action To Curb Communist Propaganda

Cigar manufacturers of Tampa, representing the entire industry, decided at a mass meeting last night to discontinue reading in the factories, beginning this morning, as a means of curbing communistic agitation.

"There has been a decided feeling of unrest in the cigar industry of Tampa over a period of several months, culminating in a flame of activity since the disturbance in Ybor City on Saturday night, November 7, since which time seven of Tampa's largest factories have been called on strike. . . . At a mass meeting last night of all the cigar manufacturers of Tampa, a full discussion brought out the fact that all of the trouble is originating from the readers' stand where fiery communistic translations from anarchistic publications have been constantly poured into the workers. . . . The reading of anarchistic propaganda has caused the manufacturers to immediately withdraw the privilege of reading any matter whatsoever in the factories, and reading in all factories is to be discontinued indefinitely from this morning on." (Tampa Cigar Manufacturers' Association, November 27, 1931)

"Even in Cuba, where President Gerardo Machado rules with an iron hand, the president allows readers in the factories to read vehement denunciations of himself. Surely in this land of freedom, the manufacturers will not be less liberal." (Victoriano Manteiga, November 30, 1931)

"Cigar makers of Tampa factories held a mass meeting yesterday morning at the Labor Temple and voted a 72–hour strike that put approximately 7,000 workers on the street. . . . The walkout followed word that manufacturers had decided to discontinue reading in factories. . . . The strike vote, however, was taken as a protest against the imprisonment of seventeen alleged communist agitators. . . . During the day there was an effort to get Latin bakers, barbers, coffee shop clerks and cooks out with the cigar makers, and some members of these groups were reported to have quit." (*Tampa Morning Tribune*, November 28, 1931)

"Virtually every business house in Ybor City and West Tampa, except for drug stores and cafés, closed its doors yesterday afternoon at the request of striking cigar makers." (*Tampa Morning Tribune*, November 29, 1931)

A mass meeting of Tampa cigar workers on November 28, 1931, protesting the removal of readers from the factories.

"Recognizing the economic situation in the city, the cigar manufacturers . . . will gladly reopen the factories for employment of such employees as they possibly take care of at this time, provided the factories can be operated upon a basis of true Americanism and loyalty to our city, state and federal government. . . . The factories will not permit reading in the plants nor will any speeches whatsoever be permitted." (Tampa Cigar Manufacturers' Association, December 7, 1931)

"1,500 cigar workers voted at a mass meeting at the Labor Temple yesterday to drop all strike demands and return to work on whatever terms the manufacturers might be willing to take them back." (*Tampa Morning Tribune*, December 11, 1931)

"Yesterday approximately seventy percent of the number that went on strike were back at work. Reds had been weeded out, and the faithful workers . . . were on the job." (*Tobacco Leaf,* December 19, 1931)

THE TOBACCO LEAF for December 19, 1931

70 Percent Of Striking Cigarmakers Back At Work

Red Leaders Excepted, Tampa Manufacturers Take Back Large Portion of Workers Under Specific Rulings—Speeches, Collections and Readers Barred—No Wage Reduction Mentioned—Industry Again On Sound Basis and in Good Spirits

Manuel Aparicio, a lector, lost his job when manufacturers permanently banned reading in 1931.

"Because we read and disseminated the labor press, we incurred the hostility of the factory owners. We were accused of making communist propaganda. That simply was not true. The cigar workers paid, and one had to read precisely what the cigar workers wanted. Management did not approve of this system. It was at the height of one of these controversies that they abolished the *lectura*. They removed the platform on which we sat. At this point, the workers took to the streets. . . . The *lectura* ended in 1931. After the strike, many *lectores* returned to the factories as cigar workers. And I, with a compatriot, opened a little café in Ybor." (Abelardo Gutiérrez Días, 1975)

"The strike left a psychological scar on me. I was in junior high school. . . . My mother was in the strike. . . . The 1931 strike was openly radical. By then, there was a Communist Party in Ybor City. Leaflets would be distributed by people whom you knew. (Laughs.) They'd come down the street in the car (whispers) with their headlights off. And then onto each porch. Everybody knew who it was. They'd say, 'Oh, *cómo está*, Manuel.' (Laughs.). . . . The strike was a ghastly one. When the factories opened, they cut off many workers." (Jose Yglesias, 1970)

"Widely known for his support of liberal causes benefitting Latins, Victoriano P. Manteiga was honored throughout the years for his active involvement in community and civic affairs. . . . Born in Cuba, Manteiga arrived in Florida in 1913 to build a future. With two white suits and less than ten dollars in his pocket, he immediately landed a job as a *lector* (reader) in a local cigar factory. . . . Then in 1922, with the help of his wife and the backing of others in Ybor City, he began publishing *La Gaceta*. It was then an afternoon Spanish-language daily, filled with news for the immigrant population. . . . Throughout his career, Manteiga was more interested in the literary and humanitarian aspects of publishing than in the business end. He read extensively and spent much of his time giving speeches and collecting money for anti-fascist causes like that of the Loyalists of the Republic in the Spanish Civil War. . . . Manteiga remained editor and publisher of *La Gaceta* until semi-retiring in 1961. After that, he continued writing regularly for the newspaper until about three years before he died in 1982." (*Tampa Times*, August 2, 1982)

"Mr. Manteiga was a terribly impressive man. . . . When Manteiga walked into a room, he was always recognized as someone who had stature and importance." (César Medina, 1982)

Victoriano Manteiga (1895–1982), founder and long-time editor of La Gaceta, *an Ybor City institution since 1922. (Courtesy of* La Gaceta)

A typical front page of La Gaceta in 1922 featured news stories from Madrid, Washington, Moscow, and Havana.

*Members of the Tampa Committee to Aid Spanish War Suffers posing with 6,000
pounds of boxed clothing ready to ship to Spain (1937).*

"I remember the reaction of the community to the Spanish Civil War (1936–39). In
1931 elections, Spain had shown that the Monarchy had lost in local and parliamen-
tary elections, and Alfonso XIII abdicated and left Spain. The Second Spanish Republic was established. . . . The Ybor community, living here under a constitutional republic, welcomed the Spanish Republic. . . . In 1936, the military rose against the
Republic, and a civil war ensued that lasted three bloody years. In the end the Republic was abolished. The great majority of the Ybor population had backed the Republic
and were against the overthrow of the elected government by the military. Locally,
meetings were held in support of the Republic, activities were held to raise money,
ambulances were purchased, food was collected and sent to Spain, and several men
left to join the Lincoln Brigade to fight for the Republic. The people listened daily to
the BBC and to shortwave radio from Spain. The clubs were centers of support for the
Republic. Although the Italian dictator Mussolini sent troops to fight against the Republic, most members of the Italian community sided with the Republic. . . . These
were exciting times which galvanized the community." (Braulio Alonso, 1997)

"The total community was with Loyalist Spain. They used to send enormous
amounts of things. It was totally organized." (Jose Yglesias, 1970)

"The minute that we knew there was a war on, and how bad it was going for the people, not for the military, but for the people that were not in power. And it was really going real bad for them. So everybody started, as they always do when somebody is in trouble, they all go to help the person that is in trouble. And of course, the bigger the war got, and the fighting, the worse it got. Then we knew that it wasn't enough just to listen to what was happening and be interested, that we had to help. So that's when everybody started to help. All the clubs here in Tampa, they started to help." (Alice Menéndez, 1997)

"My father wasn't a communist or a socialist, he was just a Republican. He had the ideas of a democratic government like they have over here. He had been exposed to this and he liked it. And that's what he wanted—a democracy. And he figured the Republic, the Republicans were the ones to give it." (Aída P. González, 1997)

A meeting at the Centro Asturiano in support of the Spanish Republic with Alfonso Coniglio (left) and Vincent Antinori (center), secretary of the Italian Club.

"Usually when they got together at the Labor Temple [which served as headquarters for Tampa's Democratic Popular Committee to Aid Spain], many times the whole auditorium was full. And, many times, people standing in the back, they couldn't get a seat. . . . The whole community came together. Very much so. Mainly through word of mouth, through the cigar factories. And also at the time there used to be these panel trucks with the loudspeakers. They'd go up and down the neighborhoods, with the loudspeakers, maybe announcing a meeting that was coming. . . . And the people would just line up." (Amelia B. Menéndez, 1997)

"The clubs started to have different kinds of benefits, plays and picnics—all kinds of things that they had to make money. And they did make a lot of money. . . . According to the size of the city, we did as much, if not more, than other bigger cities with bigger populations." (Alice Menéndez, 1997)

Ybor City's current Labor Temple on Eighth Avenue, which opened in 1934, housed offices for cigar worker unions and included an auditorium for public meetings. (Courtesy of Florida State Archives)

Tickets from a stub-book certifying the amount donated to Tampa's Democratic Popular Committee to Aid Spain. (Courtesy of Ana Varela-Lago)

"Saturday afternoon I made the runs of the cigar factories in Tampa. . . . The entrance is usually one-story high with an ample stone staircase. At the bottom of the stairs, or at the landing, were people assigned to make the collections. With a stub-book in their hands, they handed over a ticket for the amount of the contribution made. From the factory came men and women, Latins and Americans, blacks and whites. 'For Spanish Democracy! For Spanish Democracy!' cried out the bearers of the stub-book. There was no worker who did not contribute something. But the donations were not given as one gives alms, or meets an obligation, or pays a tax, or bears a heavy tribute with resignation; they were given with the expression, demeanor, and tone of one who proudly fulfills a higher duty. In one of those cigar factories I shook the hand of a humble worker who, from the beginning of the war, has donated five dollars every week. In another cigar factory, I was introduced to a woman who gives to Spain as much money as she used to save." (Marcelino Domingo, 1938)

"I remember the collections that they used to make at the steps of the cigar factories . . . and when cigar makers came out of the cigar factories, they always had a quarter or fifty cents, or whatever they felt they could afford. . . . I believe they also collected enough to where they were able to buy four ambulances that also went to Spain." (Angel Rañón, 1997)

"The cigar workers where my mother worked in García & Vega got together and they formed a committee, and they said: 'Let's have a march to protest, and ask [President] Roosevelt to lift the embargo and to help the poor children that are suffering in Spain.' And it was organized in the Labor Temple in Ybor City, and we marched from there down to City Hall. . . . It was a very impressive demonstration." (Joe C. Maldonado, 1997)

"The first political demonstration that I can remember was a march from Ybor City and the Centro Obrero [Labor Temple] to downtown Tampa to support the Republic. I wasn't quite seven years old. There were women standing on porches and applauding and cheering and waving. And the chant was 'Lift the embargo against Loyalist Spain.'" (Willie García, 1997)

A demonstration in support of the Spanish Republic organized by women cigar workers in May 1937.

Women operating bunch-making machines at the Regensburg factory (c. 1917).

"About twenty years ago (c. 1917), a number of the cigar factories in Ybor City began to install machines for performing certain operations in the making of cigars. The use of machines has increased since that time and as a consequence a large number of cigar workers have been permanently thrown out of employment. Each machine eliminates from eight to fifteen hand workers." (Federal Writers' Project, 1937)

"Most of the cigar-making machines in Tampa—and there's more of it than the workers know of and more than I know of—are here as a result of mistaken demands by workers. This much has been accomplished: the cigar manufacturer knows that machines will make good, popular priced cigars, and machines won't strike. In other words, mistaken demands by workers have brought machines to Tampa." (*Tobacco Leaf,* June 18, 1927)

"There is not an employee of Hav-A-Tampa that is from Ybor City. All their employees are women who come from little towns near Tampa. The factory is situated here in Ybor City, yet very few Latins, if any, are employed. This factory pays their employees whatever they please." (John [Giovanni] Cacciatore, 1936)

"We still have a very large number of cigar makers out of work in Tampa. . . . At present over 2,500 are out of work. There are between 90 and 100 automatic machines, and countless numbers of different kinds of bunch-making machines. We also have quite a number of banding machines, and of stripping machines." (*Cigar Makers' Official Journal*, May and September 1929)

"The relief committee of cigar makers and strippers continues to distribute rations to increasing numbers that are unemployed." (*Cigar Makers' Official Journal*, July 1930)

Stripping machines at the Hav-A-Tampa factory removed the stem from the tobacco leaf, a task previously done by hand.

Cigar workers in front of West Tampa's W. T. Morgan factory (1936) with Josephine Rey (far left) and her young daughter Dolores. (Courtesy of Dolores Rey Partie)

"In the factory I work in now, I make thirty cents an hour but it's not regular work all the time. The days we are working we make about two dollars and thirty cents. . . . We used to make fifty-five dollars a week, but now nobody makes much more than about eighteen dollars. I guess it's mostly because the machines can make cigars so cheap; you can buy the best kind of cigar now, two for five cents. And ain't nobody smoking cigars like they used to; young people are all smoking cigarettes. Cigars is going out of style." ("Enrique," 1939)

"To my manner of thinking, the cigar-making machines are at the root of all the evil in Ybor City. They have gradually displaced the cigar makers. As an example, the factory of Santaella installed five machines, and threw out thirty cigar makers." (Fernando Lemos, 1936)

CIGAR MAKERS INTERNATIONAL UNION OF AMERICA

JOINT ADVISORY BOARD
TAMPA, FLORIDA

LABOR TEMPLE
1614 EIGHTH AVENUE

P. O. BOX 5359
YBOR CITY STATION

The letterhead of Tampa union locals affiliated with the Cigar Makers' International Union, which won recognition and a contract for most Tampa cigar workers in 1933.

"[In the 1930s] I helped organize the union along with many other cigar workers who were suffering because of the abuses the employers and henchmen committed. There were no benefits of any kind for the workers. They had no job protection, vacations, seniority, or holidays. There was no job security. Sometimes people reported to work to find that they had no jobs, just because someone took a notion to get rid of them. No previous notice was given. In many cases people had to pay, underhanded, a portion of their pay to someone in order to keep their jobs. . . . We were told, 'Organize yourselves and demand changes in the system.' Since I was so poor, I went along with that. Believe you me, they were not too far off base when they said that, because organizing is the only way down-trodden people can get anything from the powers that be. . . . President Franklin Delano Roosevelt . . . and the New Dealers put a stop to all that and enacted many laws beneficial to the working people. Boy, did we need them." (Frank D. Diez, 1989)

"The average monthly payroll during the years up to about 1929 was about $1,600,000. The estimated payroll in 1937–38 has been about $800,000 to $900,000 monthly. While the production in Tampa during the past ten years does not show a startling decrease in the number of cigars produced, the reduction in the value of production is startling indeed. Production value has decreased as a result of demand for cheaper cigars. . . . The industry was organized upon all Havana [tobacco] and hand labor. . . . During the past few years there has been a complete change in these conditions until today about 65 percent of the cigars manufactured sell for five cents and less than 35 percent retail at ten cents and up. This condition is doubtless due to the necessity for economy on the part of the American public in general and to the popularity which has been attained by the five-cent cigar. The manufacture of the all-Havana, hand-made cigar was an art and is still considered so. . . . However, with the introduction of machinery and other modifications in the method of manufacture, it has been necessary for the Tampa manufacturer to attempt to meet this competition."
(*Tampa Daily Times,* December 29, 1938)

Tampa cigar workers (c. 1927)

"I went to New York by car in 1936. . . . My brother Jose came in 1937 after he graduated from high school." (Dalia Corro, 2002)

"People began to go off to New York to look for jobs. Almost all my family were in New York in 1937. You'd take that bus far to New York. There, we all stayed together. . . . People would show up from Tampa, and you'd put them up. . . . Some would drift back as jobs would open up again in Tampa." (Jose Yglesias, 1970)

"Due to the lack of employment it is said that between 2,500 and 3,000 cigar workers have left Ybor City and West Tampa [since 1932]. Most of them went to New York and some returned to Cuba, but it is estimated that at least 3,000 are still idle in Tampa." (Federal Writers' Project, 1937)

"There is not much hope in Ybor City. . . . The people of Ybor City are orphans, not only of father and mother, but of everything in life. They cannot find work at the cigar factories because of the machines. . . . Under the present conditions the people of Ybor City have no other alternative but to leave for New York City." (John [Giovanni] Cacciatore, 1936)

Jose Yglesias and his sister Dalia, an unemployed cigar maker, went to New York City in search of jobs during the 1930s. (Courtesy of Dalia Corro)

The directors of the Cuban Club (1937), posing before portraits of (left to right) Ignacio Agramonte (leader of the Ten Years War), José Martí, and Tomás Estrada Palma (first president of the Cuban Republic, 1902–1906). (Courtesy of La Gaceta)

"The Círculo Cubano is now going through a period of hard trials due to the poor business conditions which have decreased its membership to nearly one-half of what it was, as the members could not pay their weekly dues. These conditions began with the installing of machines to make cigars which put a lot of able men out of work. Besides those that remained working earned minimum wages which were not enough to cover their most urgent necessities. . . . Another reason the membership of the organization has decreased is that a large number of people left and are still leaving for New York. . . . It is necessary for the Cuban Club to celebrate festivals every month to cover the deficits which occur because expenses are not covered due to the arrears in dues of members." (Federal Writers' Project, 1937)

"The effect of the Depression on Florida's Latins was truly terrible." (Stetson Kennedy, 1942)

"In 1935 the canteen reverberated with men's talk and laughter and the clacking noise of dominoes in play. The Depression did not keep cigar makers from the cafés. They simply did not spend. They refused offers of coffee and pastry and cognac—to reciprocate was a matter of pride—or pretended that at last they had broken themselves of these habits and of the vice of playing the numbers." (Jose Yglesias, 1971)

The canteen of the Centro Asturiano (1941).

Ybor City's Seventh Avenue in 1937.

"Ybor City, as a whole, is a Latin community where a large number of the inhabitants have not become American citizens. The government, both national and local, has done very little toward making the Cuban people, as well as the other Latin nationalities, feel that they are Americans. Even many of the second and third generations of the Cubans, although born in the United States, and by right of the Constitution [are] Americans, are not considered as Americans by many of the English-speaking Americans. Many of the English-speaking Americans (who have never associated with the Latins) are biased against them without any cause whatsoever." (Federal Writers' Project, 1935)

Students at West Tampa's A. L. Cuesta School. (Courtesy of La Gaceta)

"It was difficult. You would speak English in school—you felt like you had to be-cause you didn't want to be ostracized from the other kids or be different from them, and because the teachers would punish you and reprimand you if they heard you speaking the language. But when you came home, you had to speak Spanish or Italian if you wanted to communicate with your parents and grandparents. It's a blessing now to be bilingual. But then, it was confusing to us and to our elders. . . . We lived in two worlds—a Latin world that was very ordered and traditional, and an American world that was rapidly changing and didn't really understand us or try to understand us." (Jorge García, 1977)

"Tampa teachers must not inflict corporal punishment upon Latin-American young-sters who converse with their playmates on the school grounds in languages other than English, trustees of the [Hillsborough County] school district agreed yesterday. . . . However, the trustees' instructions that principals and teachers must 'discourage as much as possible' the speaking of any language other than English on school property will remain in effect. The trustees banned corporal punishment during their discussion of a complaint that a pupil at Cuesta elementary school was spanked or whipped for speaking Spanish." (*Tampa Morning Tribune,* September 27, 1944)

"Tampa is having a rather quiet Christmas season, what with the war and all. . . . While some social activities were canceled in Tampa because of the war, leaders in the Latin colony decided that play is as important as work, and that the war effort must be maintained. However, the coronation of a queen, an annual affair at Centro Asturiano, was called off. . . . Throughout the city the management and workers of Tampa cigar factories are cooperating in buying defense bonds and Tampa's Latin clubs are taking a lead in heavy purchases. Many of these bonds are being bought through union locals." (*Tobacco Leaf,* January 3, 1942)

"This old-fashioned town appears this week to be digging out of most of its troubles, and if it just had a few cigars to meet the avalanche of orders, there'd be merry Christmas for all. . . . In the past, the industry has had all the labor it needed, but not now. A good cigar maker is a jewel, and more and more they are quitting their benches to help make ships." (*Tobacco Leaf,* November 21, 1942)

"ALUMINIO USADO AQUI!" *During World War II, Tampa's Latin community collected scrap aluminum to support the war effort.*

Friends, including Roland Manteiga (second from left), posed in Ybor City before going off to war (1943). (Courtesy of La Gaceta)

Evaldo (left) and Florencio Alfonso (right) with their father Arturo (a Tampa cigar maker) and a nephew during World War II. (Courtesy of Dalia Corro)

"Every man, just as every city, should be prepared to face the horror of war. Every man in Tampa, as well as in New York, should comprehend the enormity of the danger facing our nation." (*La Gaceta*, December 12, 1941)

Jose Yglesias, the son of cigar makers, volunteered for the U. S. Navy during World War II. (Courtesy of Dalia Corro)

"The draft board had classified me 3A because I was my mother's support, but I volunteered anyway because I believed in the war, in the popular front against fascism, in the New Deal, in socialism and the brotherhood of man—it made me unique in the aviation unit, the entire cruiser." (Jose Yglesias, 1988)

Tampa cigar makers in 1950.

"In 1949, only 7,000 people were employed in Tampa's cigar industry although they produced the same number of cigars as had 13,000 workers twenty years previously. Competition caused the death of many small cigar concerns (buckeyes). There were a total of 159 tobacco firms in 1927 and only 18 in 1949." (*Tampa Tribune Florida Accent,* December 14, 1969)

"Still noted primarily for its cigar factories, Ybor City turns out more than 40,000,000 cigars monthly. . . . In recent years the number of cigar workers has declined as factories have turned more and more to machines, but the output has increased. The 'finest cigars in the world' is still the boast of Ybor City and many factories still take pride in the taste and perfection of the hand-made cigar." (*Tampa Tribune,* November 14, 1951)

Machines run largely by women dominated the Tampa cigar industry by the 1950s. (Courtesy of Florida State Archives)

"A great many cigar workers made cigars by hand up until World War II. That's when machines, which had existed for decades, came into wide use in Tampa. 'The machine came in, and progress put everybody out of work,' says Bertha Peláez." (*Tampa Tribune*, December 9, 1990)

"When the machines came, somebody came to me and told me they are using some machines for the cheap cigars. This man said, 'Don't tell nobody, but go when you are finished working, go and learn the machine. They are going to fire lots of people.' And they did fire lots of people. Even him. Then the competition came. Everybody wanted to learn the machine. It was scary. That machine ran." (Dolores Río, 1987)

"One machine displaces twenty workers. A fast, good man can make 125 cigars a day; a machine turns out 4,000 a day." (*Miami Herald*, February 8, 1959)

"Although technology has taken over in many places, the cigar maker is much the same now as he always was, and the product he makes is still the best to be had. . . . During the fiscal year ended June 30, 1955, 681,021,000 cigars were made in Tampa. Eleven percent of all the cigars made in the United States were made in Tampa. This was the largest percentage of any year in the history of the industry. . . . Tampa's cigar industry gives employment to some 5,500 people with a payroll of $12,500,000 a year. . . .

"The cigar makers themselves have given the Tampa cigar something that only Tampa has—an expertness in his trade, a feeling for tradition and a mature tobacco sense. . . . Unfortunately, the ancient art of hand-making cigars is fast dying out. Very few young men are taking up the trade, and out of approximately 10,000 who worked here twenty-five years ago, only about 2,500 are left. Women now run the machines for the most part. But the old-time cigar maker each week still turns out many thousands of the finest cigars made in the world." (*Tampa Tribune*, October 30, 1955)

The hand system (with molds) was still used by some cigar makers in 1954, including Philomena Leone (far right), who came to Tampa from Sicily at the age of six in 1913 and worked most of her life as a cigar maker. (Courtesy of James Leone)

"Strangely enough, it is often difficult for a factory to find enough hand-made cigar workers to fill the benches. The art of cigar making is slowly dying with the advent of the machine." (*Tampa Tribune,* November 25, 1956)

"Each year there are fewer and fewer of the nimble-fingered cigar makers who labor painstakingly at their benches, with press and mold, and produce the fine cigars for which Tampa is famous. . . . The real expensive shapes, cigars selling for thirty-five cents and up, still must be made by hand because no machine yet can duplicate these fancy shapes. . . . Machines will never match nicety of workmanship, nicety of packing the filler." (*Miami Herald,* February 8, 1959)

Tampa cigar workers in the 1960s.

An aging packer in a Tampa factory. (Courtesy of Florida State Archives)

"Some jobs will never be taken over by machines—especially when it comes to producing the kind of cigars Tampa makers boast about. For instance, the packers and selectors. There are thirty-two shades of Havana tobacco ranging from light green to dark brown—and the men who pack the boxes must have an acute eye for each shade. Each cigar in a box must be of the same color. . . . Probably no other industry has so high an age level—an average of fifty-eight. One finds hundreds of skilled workers in their sixties and seventies. The oldest cigar maker, a true venerable of the trade, is eighty. He is Manuel Gutiérrez, spry and agile at his bench, who started working as a boy of fifteen with the Sánchez y Haya plant." (*Miami Herald,* February 8, 1959)

"A shortage which manufacturers see as a continuing problem is the need for more packers, shippers and wrapper selectors. These are key positions, and replacements for those who retire because of age or disability are not readily available." (*Tobacco Leaf,* November 10, 1956)

"Tampa's Latin-American flavor is strongly evident in the thirty-six cigar factories in this city. Spanish is the language of the trade, and in some of the larger factories there may be as many as a hundred workers in one room all chatting in Spanish and shaping cigars by hand just as Ybor's workers did in the 1880s." (*New York Times,* December 18, 1960)

"Today 70 percent of all the workers in Tampa's cigar industry are women. Fifty percent of these women are past the age of forty-five. The average age is about fifty-five years of age, according to figures available at the Cigar Makers' Union. It is estimated 50 percent of the women are the main source of income in the home. A little over 50 percent of the workers have only a sixth-grade education; 36 percent speak little or no English. The large majority of these women are married and their husbands are working. The combined income of the husband and wife has been one of the chief factors in raising the standard of living of the cigar workers. . . . A large majority of the women in the upper age brackets have a very small amount of formal education. They started working in the factories when they were twelve to sixteen years old and have been at it every since. All they know is how to make cigars." (*Tampa Tribune,* May 28, 1962)

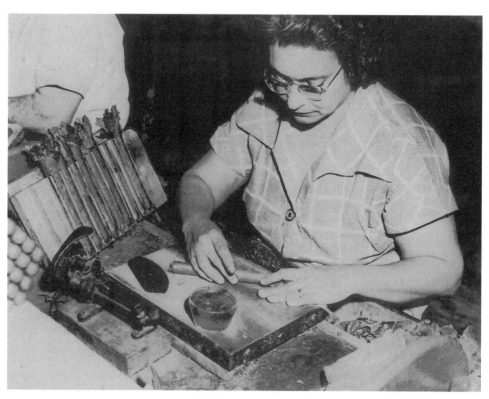

A cigar maker at the Cuesta-Rey factory. (Courtesy of Nonita Cuesta-Henson)

Afro-Cuban women stripping stems from tobacco leaves in preparation for making cigars at home (c. 1960).

"Twelve major and sixty-five small factories are in existence now. Many of the small factories are homegrown affairs employing as few as two workers. Years ago Ybor City and West Tampa were dotted with about 150 factories—but none had the production capacities found in big factories today." (*Miami Herald*, February 8, 1959)

"The so-called buckeye shops employ from two to twenty people. The buckeyes still turn out the hand-made cigars for which Tampa was famous across the world." (*Tampa Tribune*, September 5, 1965)

Tampa's 26th of July Club was organized in 1955 to support Fidel Castro. (Courtesy of La Gaceta)

"The cry of Cuba Libre will be raised again in Tampa, as it has so many times in the past, Sunday afternoon . . . when a young Cuban revolutionary is scheduled to make a speech against the regime of Fulgencio Batista. The revolutionary is Fidel Castro, a twenty-nine-year-old doctor of law from the University of Havana and the leader of a bloody revolt against the Cuban army in July 1953 at Santiago. . . . He is here under the auspices of a recently formed society in Tampa—the 26th of July Club." (*Tampa Morning Tribune*, November 26, 1955)

"Fidel Castro [spoke at] the CIO Hall at 1226 Seventh Avenue between Twelfth and Thirteenth Streets. . . . Groups of anti-Batista Tampans and followers of Castro roamed about Ybor City stirring up interest in this afternoon's meeting. It created an old-time revolutionary atmosphere with groups of rapidly speaking, heavily mustachioed young Cuban-Americans congregating on street corners and making plans." (*Tampa Morning Tribune*, November 27, 1955)

"Fidel Castro, young Cuban revolutionary, yesterday promised an Ybor City audience to fight to the death, to free his country from what he called the dictatorship of President Fulgencio Batista. . . . Castro praised Tampa and Tampans. 'The Republic of Cuba is the daughter of the cigar makers of Tampa,' he declared. As for his revolution, he said he could not disclose his plans, and he quoted José Martí, the apostle of Cuba: 'The results are public, but the methods are secret.'" (*Tampa Morning Tribune*, November 28, 1955)

Fidel Castro (second from right) during his 1955 visit to Tampa.

UNITED STATES

Tobacco Journal

Vol. 177 — No. 6   February 8, 1962

U. S. Bans Imports of Cuban Tobacco

★ ## Industry Facing Crisis In Curb on Havana Leaf

Worst Problems May Be a Year or Two Away, Trade Leaders Indicate; Corral of Tampa Ass'n And Weiner of CMA Assess Effects of Embargo

The complete prohibition of imports of Cuban tobacco into the United States will create serious problems for a major part of the cigar industry in this country, but the worst of these problems may not arise for a year or two, trade leaders indicated this week.

James J. Corral, vice president-general manager of Corral, Wodiska y Ca., of Tampa, Fla., and president of the Tampa Cigar Manufacturers' Association, declared that the industry's situation is "going to be very, very difficult" if Cuban leaf becomes completely unavailable, because "There are no substitutes to produce the kind of cigars we are making."

Among the major domestic cigar manufacturers, Stanley S. Keyser, president of Consolidated Cigar Corp., and Julius Strauss, president of General Cigar Co., each indicated that his company's anticipation of the embargo had enabled plans to be made for

handling the situation without any interruption in output or any relaxation of current high standards of quality.

Dr. Clarence M. Weiner, economist of the Cigar Manufacturers' Association of America, said in reference to the anticipated disappearance of Havana tobacco from American cigar blends that alternative sources of supply may be used on a larger scale, and that the existence of substantial stocks of Cuban leaf in this country will give manufacturers time to change their blends so gradually that most smokers will not notice the difference.

Mr. Corral, explaining that Tampa manufacturers now engaged in production of clear Havana cigars probably would try to use domestic tobacco when their inventories of Cuban leaf have

(Continued on Page 5)

★ ## Embargo Set By President; Seek Job Aid

Legislation Sought to Ease Impact of End of Imports of Cigar Leaf

WASHINGTON, D. C., Sunday — A complete embargo against imports of Cuban products into the United States was ordered yesterday by President John F. Kennedy.

The ban on Cuban imports — including recently dwindling but still important shipments of cigar tobacco — will be placed in effect at 12:01 A. M. (EST) on Wednesday, February 7.

President Kennedy's action was taken under the Foreign Assistance Act of 1961, instead of under the Trading With the Enemy Act. This move is understood to be designed to exert the maximum economic pressure against the Cuban government of Premier Fidel Castro, without the necessity of "freezing" the assets of

(Continued on Page 5)

"The Cuban tobacco embargo hit Tampa today. . . . Hardest hit by the embargo starting today were Tampa's smaller firms turning out hand-rolled cigars of pure Havana leaf. Of Tampa's thirty-four cigar manufacturers some twelve fall in this category." (*Tampa Times*, February 7, 1962)

"In the nearly four months since the blow of the embargo on Cuban tobacco landed on Tampa . . . the pessimism of cigar workers has deepened to the point of despair. Their hearts are gripped by the icy fingers of fear as they look forward to the day when they will have no jobs and no place to turn. The latest count made by the Florida Employment Service shows that 754 cigar workers are now receiving unemployment compensation. At least 200 others are working at whatever kind of job they can get for whatever pay, and as day laborers they are not making much. . . . The cigar makers blamed the embargo on Cuban tobacco for all their ills. . . . They feel the government owes them something for taking their jobs away." (*Tampa Tribune*, May 27, 1962)

"The final blow came with the revolution in Cuba. You could not make first-rate cigars without tobacco from the Vuelta Abajo area of Pinar del Río. . . . For the old-timers the embargo was further proof of the barbarity of *americanos*." (Jose Yglesias, 1977)

"Presently there are only two or three Tampa cigar companies that specialize in making hand-rolled cigars. Automation has extended its steel fingers into that specialized industry, and it's slowly dying out." (*Tampa Times*, February 9, 1976)

"Tampa's cigar factories, many deserted or converted, produced as many memories as cigars. . . . In 1964, cigar sales nationwide peaked at 9.3 billion cigars. In 1981, that number was reduced to just under 3.4 billion. . . . Even though the number of Tampa cigar factories has shrunk dramatically . . . Arturo Fuente's business is a good example of a local manufacturer who is benefitting from increased sales of premium, high-priced cigars, an increase which is helping to support the industry in spite of overall losses. . . . The Fuente factory in Tampa is currently on the receiving end of hand-made cigars from Santo Domingo. . . . 'We've cut production in Tampa, but we've gained, expanding production in Santo Domingo,' says Arturo Fuente, current vice president and son of the founder of Arturo Fuente Cigar Co." (*Tampa Tribune*, July 9, 1982)

Ybor City in the 1970s, showing a boarded-up cigar factory.

HOW TO WIN FRIENDS AND INFLUENCE TOURISTS

A cartoon from the Tampa Sunday Tribune, *December 11, 1949.*

"Restoration of Ybor City into the nation's outstanding attraction of its kind with a Pan American plaza, international trade mart, a monument to Cuba's national hero, a hotel, apartments, shops, and other business buildings was suggested yesterday as a possible goal for Tampa." (*Tampa Morning Tribune,* July 17, 1949)

"There will always be an Ybor City, BUT—

"Whether it becomes a thing of pride—and profit—to all of Tampa, or whether it becomes a sinkhole of slums to avoid with loathing, is being decided right now, in the opinion of many section leaders. . . . Ybor City might be developed to the point that Tampa would join the list of major tourist attractions in the nation's greatest tourist state. Tony Pizzo, a dreamer of that dream, says, 'Tampa is being by-passed by tourists. Yet we have potentially one of the greatest attractions—the only foreign quarter in the state, or in the Southeast.'" (*Tampa Daily Times,* October 8, 1958)

"Ybor City is the only important piece of land we [in Hillsborough County] have. It can rival Disney World." (Armando Valdés, Jr., 1969)

"Ybor City has never been so divided. The colorful Latin section of Tampa is practically bisected by a two-block trip of desolation, site of future spans making up Interstate Highway No. 4. Most of the north-south roads are cut off by the plowed-up right-of-way. Heavy earth-moving machinery has replaced the jam-packed row-on-row of small houses. . . .

"'I lost many customers who used to live out there,' a grocer said, pointing to the barren road site. 'Were there any grocery stores out there?' he was asked. 'Out there where the road will be? Yes,' he said, 'One.' 'Well, maybe you got that store's customers,' it was suggested. 'Oh, no,' he said. 'Customers are not like that. Customers come in every day and buy something. They buy on credit. And they come from within a block away, do you see? Maybe I got one more customer from the store that was moved. But almost half my customers lived on the other side of the street where the road came through.'" (*Tampa Tribune*, June 3, 1962)

The junction of Interstate 4 and Interstate 275, as it neared completion in 1963, showing Interstate 4 splitting Ybor City in the background. Interstate 275 skirted downtown Tampa but cut through the old section of West Tampa, dividing it in two.

Ybor City houses built for cigar workers and located on Sixteenth Street.

"After World War II, Ybor City first began to deteriorate noticeably. . . . Financing from the GI Bill of Rights prompted many young Latins who'd served during World War II to migrate from Ybor City to upgraded West Tampa neighborhoods. Between 1950 and 1960, the area's black population had risen 38 percent, and prejudices that had been directed against Ybor since the gangster era of the '30s and '40s increased with the awareness that Latins were moving out and blacks were moving in. 'The City Within a City,' as its dwindling Latin citizenry called it, was largely in the 1960s a crumbling mess of inferior housing. Wooden 'shotgun houses,' constructed for cigar factory workers fifty, sixty, or seventy years earlier, were crunched together on narrow streets like dilapidated shoe boxes. Some Latin home sites were maintained with cleanliness and pride, it's true, but most structures were obviously substandard. . . .

"Adjacent to the commercial district, north of Seventh Avenue, was the sadly crumbling residential neighborhood where Ybor's cigar-producing citizenry had lived and bred for three-quarters of a century. In 1965, home sites there, including many 'shotgun houses,' numbered more than 660; approximately 1,100 families lived in the thirty-square block area. It was here that, among other improvements, Urban Renewal proposed erecting low-income, multi-family housing. The plan was to relocate the Latin residents—many of whom were elderly—tear down the neighborhood, attract developers to build housing, then invite the people back again. In so doing, Urban Renewal would 'revitalize' the area and Ybor City would be 'reborn.'" (*Tampa Tribune,* May 13, 1979)

"What Tampa's Urban Renewal office proposed to do in Ybor City in 1965—after three years of extensive planning—seemed simple. In plain black and white, the agency outlined its idea to 'rehabilitate, clear and redevelop slum areas' and 'preserve and strengthen the distinctive qualities . . . of Tampa's Latin heritage and present-day Latin community.'

"In feasibility studies, the consultants concluded that low-cost, multi-family housing was imperative for Ybor. They also recommended that a 'deliberate program be established to encourage and serve the tourist and regional markets' that would surely be attracted to the scene. . . . Everybody was excited about Jim Walter's proposed 'Walled City,' an enclosed five-and-one-half-acre, Spanish-style tourist attraction with staged 'bloodless bullfights' and authentic fiesta entertainment which supposedly would generate more than $20 million in annual revenues for investors, who believed the attraction would rival Busch Gardens as a tourist-grabber. And Urban Renewal, the agency with the wherewithal and the bulldozers, was going to make this all possible—help make Ybor City the Latin jewel of the South." (*Tampa Tribune,* May 13, 1979)

Eighth Avenue, looking west from Nineteenth Street, in the early 1960s before Urban Renewal.

"Go to Ybor City today and ask anybody what Urban Renewal did for his neighbor-hood in the 1960s and the local citizen—a shopkeeper, a sandwich maker, a city em-ployee or a retired cigar worker—will tell you Urban Renewal ripped apart the fabric of Ybor and threw it to the winds. Armando Valdez, for instance, an Ybor jeweler for thirty-two years, will tell you representatives from Tampa's Urban Renewal agency came in and pledged that people living in Ybor would be moved from their homes, then brought back. 'People were moved out, all right,' he will say. And their homes were destroyed. 'But who came back?' he will ask. 'Where are the people?' Valdez will scoff, then tell you Urban Renewal shattered the flow of life in 'The City Within a City' by purchasing most of Ybor's core district, bulldozing the area, then allowing the land to 'be a desert.' And he will tell you that whether it was the agency's fault or not, Urban Renewal 'sold the Latin community a bill of goods by making promises it couldn't keep.' . . .

"Now, more than a decade later, what people basically remember about Urban Re-newal in Ybor City is that the bulldozers rumbled through and pushed more than 1,100 families from their homes. . . . There is no 'Walled City' and instead of homes for Vincente Martínez Ybor's cigar workers and their descendants, there is a great, weedy deserted plain of rubble in Ybor City." (*Tampa Tribune*, May 13, 1979)

Ybor City's Tenth Avenue in 1972 with an abandoned cigar factory on the left.

Demolition by Urban Renewal on Ybor City's Eighth Avenue during 1965.

"On the very day in 1966 that an Urban Renewal official told José Vega Díaz and his wife that the couple would have to move from Ybor City, Blanca, Díaz's wife, died of sorrow. She died because the couple had lived in their small, palm-shaded house at Thirteenth Avenue and Sixteenth Street for more than fifty years. But the man from Urban Renewal told her she'd have to gather her houseplants and go. The home with the wide porch where her daughter was born would be rubble before summer was over. Blanca stood in front of a window and wept, Díaz recalls now. She was broken-hearted and could not speak but to sob, 'I can't, I can't, I can't.' . . . Before the sun was down that day, Blanca was gone, dead of a heart attack." (*Tampa Tribune*, May 13, 14, 1979)

"I didn't want to sell my house. It was a beautiful house. I took care of my house very carefully. It was okay in the afternoons when we sat on our porch and looked at the neighborhood. I remember that I planted two date palms in the front yard the day we moved in. It was 1916. The carpenter had just built the house. I designed it and he built it. It cost me $2,000. I planted the two trees and they grew very beautiful. They were our trees and they grew as my family grew. Now there is nothing where my house was except two palm trees." (José Vega Díaz, 1979)

Ybor City in 1972, as viewed from Tenth Avenue (looking southwest) with the Labor Temple on the right and the Centro Español on the left.

"Ybor City is beginning to look like it did when Mr. Ybor first came here." (Tony Pizzo, 1969)

"When the first idea of Urban Renewal was created, the intentions were basically good. But no one really considered the men and women whose lives were embedded in the community. The demolition crews are not only tearing down worn buildings but they are also destroying the once colorful dreams of hard-working men and women." (Carmen L. Caltagirone, 1968)

"Ybor City looks like the deserted back lot of a movie studio. Empty storefronts and vacant lots dominate the streetscape. Many wrought-iron balconies along the main thoroughfare of Seventh Avenue are dilapidated or gone. Only 2,100 people live there now, most of them poor blacks. The government is the largest land owner. Split by an interstate highway and virtually leveled by well-meaning urban planners, Ybor City has struggled to survive broken dreams, unkept promises and an indifferent downtown power structure." (*Orlando Sentinel,* October 14, 1985)

The Centro Español cantina.

"The clubhouses Latins built in Ybor City are impressive structures. . . . The cantinas see most of the action now. The libraries, theaters and ballrooms sleep, except when an old-timer wants to read a little history, or a group rents a ballroom for an occasional dance or party. . . . Clubs report declines in membership, with the most pronounced drop seen in Círculo Cubano's membership." (*Tampa Tribune*, September 15, 1977)

"Tampa, and especially Ybor City, has been a paella of nationalities from the beginning, but the cosmopolitan air has to an extent faded away. What made Ybor City in the past was not the architecture, it was the people, with their flair for gaiety and the sense you got of being in a foreign country when you entered the quarter." (Tony Pizzo, 1967)

"Whenever I go back to Tampa, Florida, where I was born, I spend most of my time bemoaning the breakup of its Latin section, Ybor City. . . . Only a building here and there remains of that special Latin community that was sustained by the cigar industry of hand-made, luxury Havanas." (Jose Yglesias, 1974)

"The clubs are still alive, but mostly for the old ones, like me. The young ones have other activities now. They have medical insurance in their work. . . . I'm afraid that the Italian Club and others like it will go someday—very little is being done to attract younger members." (Paul Longo, 1977)

"The majority of at least one generation of Tampans have never had any contact with the cigar industry and feel no undying ties to the culture it produced. It is not uncommon for members of the present younger generation, in spite of perhaps possessing a particularly flowery Spanish name, to be unable to speak any language but English. Through the decades, a bilingual and trilingual tradition had been an almost commonplace part of the Tampa profile. . . . Modern mobility and improved communications have been the catalyst, not only in Tampa but universally. Yet, the older generations—those old enough to have been part of the more traditional culture—appear unwilling to embrace the new life with the nonchalance of their offspring. The most mature groups adhere jealously to the Spanish and Italian ways of an older, more genteel Tampa." (*Tampa Tribune Florida Accent*, December 14, 1969)

Domino players at the Italian Club, with Tony Pizzo (standing, right) watching.

Nochebuena, an old Cuban tradition, is still observed by descendants of Tampa cigar workers like René ("Andy") Barrios (right) and his nephew Aaron Barrios Kononitz. (Photo courtesy of Maura Barrios)

"*Nochebuena.* I have never been able to find out how Christmas Eve came to be named this by Spaniards, but in Ybor City . . . it was truly a good night. Indeed, it was the best of nights. . . . When I think back about *Nochebuena* in Ybor City, I can see that although it was not a religious occasion it was certainly a reverent one. Our altar was the dinner table. All the preparations and expectations and excitement of the day led to that marvelous feast. . . .

"I was startled out of bed one Christmas Eve morning by agonized squeals coming from the backyard and ran to help whoever was in trouble. Mother yelled from the kitchen, 'Don't go there!' Too late. The men of the family were struggling with a pig. . . . The pig had to be degutted, scrubbed with boiling water, and its hair plucked, while others dug a pit for the charcoal fire. It took much work. . . . Also, many swigs from the gallon of wine. Cousin Pancho had prepared a huge pot of the *mojo,* made with sour orange juice, garlic, and paprika, and during the long hours ahead there were always two men there to turn the pig and baste it with *mojo.* . . . What made *Nochebuena* a true rite was that the menu never changed. There were (and are) no surprises in that—only confirmed delights. The menu was black beans, white rice (each grain firm and separate), sweet potatoes, yucca, salads, chicken baked in lemon and garlic sauce." (Jose Yglesias, December 1977)

"About two dozen men and women, now in their seventies, eighties and nineties, still wrap cigars by hand in Cigar City. Most work at a couple of small Ybor City factories that look like something out of a Charles Dickens novel. Heads bow over old wooden tables, each worker's station marked off by wood dividers. Their tobacco knives, called *chavetas,* scrape and chop against hard, wooden cutting boards. . . . This could be a photograph from the turn of the century." (*Tampa Tribune,* December 9, 1990)

"Only a dozen or so hand-rollers remain in Tampa. Most work in small Tampa factories, called 'buckeyes.' They're paid by the cigar, usually about $45 per thousand. If they're fast, they can make $4.50 an hour. . . . Still, their work continues for non-monetary reasons. 'You've got to keep going at my age,' Josephine Lazzara said. 'You can't sit home in a rocking chair. You'll rock yourself to death.'" (*Tampa Times,* October 14, 1991)

Tampa workers making hand-rolled cigars in the 1990s.

Tony Pizzo (1912–1994).

"I like to think of the days of my youth in Ybor City . . . recall the sights, sounds, and smells that enriched my childhood. Life was pleasant and carefree, often exciting. I can still hear the chatter in Spanish and Italian as the workers trudged light-hearted to long days of rolling cigars in the factories; the rumbling of wagons and the clump of horses' hooves through the brick streets delivering milk and loaves of bread before sunrise. I can still hear the steam-whistles of the Tampa Box Factory and the Latin-American Laundry; the Regensburg Cigar Factory tower clock striking on the hour; and the bell of Our Lady of Mercy Catholic Church calling its parishioners to mass. I cannot forget the infernal crowing of backyard roosters at the first glimmer of dawn, shattering my dreams.

"The exotic fragrances still tingle in my nostrils. I cannot forget the aroma of bread being baked by Italian housewives in their backyard ovens permeating through the neighborhood, the roasting of coffee beans in the coffee mills, creating aromatic smoke perfuming the streets, and the pungent smell of Havana tobacco being blended. . . .

"The mellifluous Latin chatter along the sidewalks in the evenings was an enchantment. I can still hear the music from the clubhouse ballrooms wafting on the night air during festive occasions. . . . The old haunts and departed friends capture my memories. It was a way of life that will not return." (Tony Pizzo, 1989)

Jose Yglesias (1919–1995) in front of the Ybor City house on Nineteenth Avenue where he grew up. (Courtesy of Florida Humanities Council)

"There is not much left of my home town. It is scattered and broken up, and its old *ambiente* seems to me almost entirely gone. I am bitterly sad about it." (Jose Yglesias, December 1977)

"In all my work as a writer I . . . tried to make American readers aware of Ybor City and its Latin cigar makers." (Jose Yglesias, 1991)

"Cigar makers provided me with an inexhaustible source of material. In any case, I had to write about them, for I feared that this community, which of necessity had to die out, would be forgotten, a part of America no one would get to know." (Jose Yglesias, 1989)

Bibliography

Abad, Joseph M. "An Ybor City Family Story." *La Gaceta,* June 27, 1997.

Aguayo, Oscar. Quoted in *Tampa Tribune,* September 14, 1977.

Alonso, Braulio. "The Ybor City I Remember." *La Gaceta,* June 27, 1997.

Alonso, Emilia González. "'Abuela Was Born Here!'" *La Gaceta,* June 27, 1997.

Alvarez, Aída. Quoted in *Tampa Tribune,* September 12, 1977.

Alvarez, José. Typescript of interview by Paul Buhle, March 15, 1983. Tamiment Library, New York University.

Aparicio, Henry. Quoted in *Tampa Tribune,* May 22, 1981.

Argintar, Sammy. Typescript of interview by Yael V. Greenberg, March 29, 2000. Copy in possession of authors.

Balbotín, B. M. "Life History of B. M. Balbotín." Typescript of interview (c. 1936) by Federal Writers' Project. Special Collections, University of South Florida Library.

Barcia Quilabert, Luis. "Autobiografía." Typescript (1957). Pizzo Collection, Special Collections, University of South Florida Library.

Bryan, Edwin L. Letter to American Civil Liberties Union, July 7, 1932. Vol. 564, ACLU Papers, Princeton University Library.

Cacciatore, John (Giovanni). "Life History of John Cacciatore." Typescript of interview (c. 1936) by Federal Writers' Project. Special Collections, University of South Florida Library.

Caltagirone, Carmen L. Letter to the editor. *Tampa Tribune,* August 11, 1968.

Campbell, A. Stuart. *The Cigar Industry of Tampa, Florida.* Gainesville: University of Florida Bureau of Economic and Business Research, 1939.

Capetillo, Luisa. Quoted in *Workers' Struggle in Puerto Rico: A Documentary History,* edited by Angel Quintero Rivera. New York: Monthly Review Press, 1976.

Castellano, Josephine. Quoted in *Living in America: One Hundred Years of Ybor City.* Film by Gayla Jamison. 1988.

Castellanos, Tony. "The Avenue." *La Gaceta,* June 27, 1997.

Cigar Makers' International Union. Quoted in *Tampa Daily Times,* November 29, 1921.

Comescone, Angelina Spoto. Quoted in *The Immigrant World of Ybor City,* by Gary R. Mormino and George E. Pozzetta. Urbana: University of Illinois Press, 1987.

Corro, Dalia. Taped interview by Robert P. Ingalls, February 5, 2002. In possession of authors.

Craparo, Rosemary Scaglione. Quoted in *The Immigrant World of Ybor City,* by Gary R. Mormino and George E. Pozzetta. Urbana: University of Illinois Press, 1987.

Díaz, Norerto. Quoted in *Palmetto Country*, by Stetson Kennedy. New York: Duell, Sloan & Pierce, 1942. Reprint, Gainesville: University Press of Florida, 1989.

Diez, Frank D. Quoted in *La Gaceta*, August 12, 1989.

Domingo, Marcelino. *El mundo ante España*. Translation by Ana Varela-Lago. Paris: La Technique du Livre, 1938.

Domínguez, Honorato Henry. Quoted in *Tampa Tribune*, September 12, 1977.

"Enrique." Typescript of interview (1939) by Federal Writers' Project. Special Collections, University of South Florida Library.

Espinosa, Emilio. Quoted in *Tampa Tribune*, September 14, 1977.

Federal Writers Project. "Social-Ethnic Study of Ybor City." Typescript (c. 1935). Special Collections, University of South Florida Library.

———. "Seeing Tampa." Typescript (c. 1937). Special Collections, University of South Florida Library.

———. "Trade Jargon." Typescript (c. 1938). Special Collections, University of South Florida Library.

———. *Florida: A Guide to the Southern-most State*. New York: Oxford University Press, 1939.

———. "Ybor City, Tampa's Latin Colony." Typescript (c. 1941). Special Collections, University of South Florida Library.

García, Jorge. Quoted in *Tampa Tribune*, September 12, 1977.

García, Pedro. Quoted in *Tampa Tribune*, September 5, 1965.

García, Willie. "El cafetero." *La Gaceta*, June 27, 1997.

———. Quoted in "'We Had to Help': Remembering Tampa's Response to the Spanish Civil War," by Ana Varela-Lago. *Tampa Bay History* 19 (Fall/Winter 1997).

Ginesta, Domingo. "Life History of Domingo Ginesta." Typescript of interview (c. 1936) by Federal Writers' Project. Special Collections, University of South Florida Library.

Giunta, Domenico. Quoted in *The Immigrant World of Ybor City*, by Gary R. Mormino and George E. Pozzetta. Urbana: University of Illinois Press, 1987.

Gómez, Máximo. Letter to Gualterio García, May 1897, in *Apuntes biográficos del Mayor General Serafín Sánchez*. Havana: Unión de Escritores y Artistas de Cuba, 1986.

González, Aída P. Quoted in "'We Had to Help': Remembering Tampa's Response to the Spanish Civil War," by Ana Varela-Lago. *Tampa Bay History* 19 (Fall/Winter 1997).

González, René. Quoted in *Tampa Tribune*, September 15, 1977.

Greenbaum, Susan D. *More Than Black: Afro-Cubans in Tampa*. Gainsville: University Press of Florida, 2002.

Grillo, Evelio. *Black Cuban, Black American: A Memoir*. Houston: Arte Públio Press, 2000.

Griñán, Sylvia. Quoted in *Tampa Tribune*, September 14, 1977.

Gutiérrez Días, Abelardo. Quoted in "Reminiscences of a *Lector*: Cuban Cigar Workers in Tampa," by Louis A. Pérez, Jr. *Florida Historical Quarterly* 53 (April 1975).

Haya, Ignacio. Quoted in *Tampa Tribune*, June 17, 1892.

Hewitt, Nancy A. *Southern Discomfort: Women's Activism in Tampa, Florida, 1880s-1920s*. Urbana: University of Illinois Press, 2001.

Hunt, H. H. Letter to George G. Wells, July 11, 1904. George Johnson Baldwin Papers, Southern Historical Collection, University of North Carolina Library.

Ingalls, Robert P. *Urban Vigilantes in the New South: Tampa, 1882–1936.* Gainesville: University Press of Florida, 1993.

Italiano, Mary Pitisci. Quoted in *The Immigrant World of Ybor City*, by Gary R. Mormino and George E. Pozzetta. Urbana: University of Illinois Press, 1987.

Kennedy, Stetson. *Palmetto Country.* New York: Duell, Sloan & Pierce, 1942. Reprint, Gainesville: University Press of Florida, 1989.

Lemos, Fernando. "Life History of Fernando Lemos." Typescript of interview (c. 1936) by Federal Writers' Project. Special Collections, University of South Florida Library.

Local 474, C.M.I.U. Quoted in *El Internacional* (Tampa), August 13, 1920.

Longo, Paul. Quoted in *Tampa Tribune*, September 15, 1977.

———. Quoted in *The Immigrant World of Ybor City*, by Gary R. Mormino and George E. Pozzetta. Urbana: University of Illinois Press, 1987.

López, Al. Quoted in *Tampa Tribune*, August 23, 1973.

———. Quoted in "Ybor City and Baseball: An Interview with Al López," by Steven F. Lawson. *Tampa Bay History*, 7 (Fall/Winter 1985).

———. Quoted in *The Immigrant World of Ybor City*, by Gary R. Mormino and George E. Pozzetta. Urbana: University of Illinois Press, 1987.

Maldonado, Joe C. Quoted in "'We Had to Help': Remembering Tampa's Response to the Spanish Civil War" by Ana Varela-Lago. *Tampa Bay History* 19 (Fall/Winter 1997).

Mallea, Juan. Quoted in *The Immigrant World of Ybor City*, by Gary R. Mormino and George E. Pozzetta. Urbana: University of Illinois Press, 1987.

Manteiga, Victoriano. Quoted in *Tampa Daily Times*, November 30 1931.

Martí, José. Quoted in "Martí in Ybor City," by Jose Yglesias. *José Martí in the United States: The Florida Experience*, edited by Louis A. Pérez. Tempe: Arizona State University Press, 1995.

Martínez, Víctor J. "Heath Care in Ybor City." *La Gaceta*, June 27, 1997.

Massari, Angelo. *The Wonderful Life of Angelo Massari, An Autobiography.* New York: Exposition Press, 1965.

Maynor, Art. "My Roots in Ybor City." *La Gaceta*, June 27, 1997.

Medina, César. Quoted in *Tampa Times*, August 4, 1982.

———. Quoted in *Living in America: One Hundred Years of Ybor City.* Film by Gayla Jamison. 1988.

Méndez, Armando. *Ciudad de Cigars: West Tampa.* Tampa: Florida Historical Society, 1994.

Menéndez, Alice. Quoted in "'We Had to Help': Remembering Tampa's Response to the Spanish Civil War," by Ana Varela-Lago. *Tampa Bay History* 19 (Fall/Winter 1997).

Menéndez, Amelia B. Quoted in "'We Had to Help': Remembering Tampa's Response to the Spanish Civil War," by Ana Varela-Lago. *Tampa Bay History* 19 (Fall/Winter 1997).

Moré, Ramón. Quoted in *La Gaceta*, March 23, 1990.

Moroni, G. Letter to Cusani Confalonieri, October 11, 1910. Box 3671, State Decimal File, Department of State Records, National Archives, Washington, D.C.

Mortellaro, James. Letter to Tony Pizzo, 1987. Pizzo Collection, Special Collections, University of South Florida Library.

Otero, Charles. Quoted in *Tampa Tribune*, September 13, 1977.

Otero, Isabel, Loretta Casellas, and Carolina Barcia. Letter to William S. Jennings, August 12, 1901. Jennings Papers, Florida State Archives, Tallahassee.

Passetti, Maria. Quoted in *Living in America: One Hundred Years of Ybor City*. Film by Gayla Jamison. 1988.

Pendas, Enrique. "Life History of Enrique Pendas." Typescript of interview (c. 1936) by Federal Writers' Project. Special Collections, University of South Florida Library.

Pérez, Louis A., Jr. "Cubans in Tampa: From Exiles to Immigrants, 1892–1901." *Florida Historical Quarterly* 53 (October 1975).

Pizzo, Tony. Quoted in *Tampa Tribune*, July 16, 1967.

———. Quoted in *Tampa Tribune Florida Accent*, December 14, 1969.

———. Quoted in *Orlando Sentinel*, November 26, 1972.

———. "Tony Pizzo's Ybor City." *Tampa Bay History* 2 (Spring/Summer 1980).

———. "El Gallego: Tampa's First Bolitero." *Sunland Tribune: The Journal of the Tampa Historical Society* 9 (1983): 33–34.

———. Quoted in *La Gaceta*, January 10, 1986.

———. Clipping from *La Gaceta*, 1989. Pizzo Collection, Special Collections, University of South Florida Library.

Poyo, Gerald E. "Tampa Cigarworkers and the Struggle for Cuban Independence." *Tampa Bay History* 7 (Fall/Winter 1985).

———. *With All, and For the Good of All: The Emergence of Popular Nationalism in the Cuban Communities of the United States, 1848–1898*. Durham, N.C.: Duke University Press, 1989.

Prende, Alfredo. Quoted in *Tampa Tribune*, September 12, 1977.

Rañón, Angel. Quoted in "'We Had to Help': Remembering Tampa's Response to the Spanish Civil War," by Ana Varela-Lago. *Tampa Bay History* 19 (Fall/Winter 1997).

Resistencia "MANIFESTO," August 1901. Microfilm of Ybor City newspapers, etc. University of South Florida Library.

Río, Dolores. Quoted in "Women in Ybor City: An Interview with a Woman Cigarworker," by Nancy A. Hewitt. *Tampa Bay History* 7 (Fall/Winter 1985).

———. Quoted in *Tampa Tribune*, February 18, 1987.

Rivero Muñiz, José. *Los cubanos en Tampa*. Havana [n. p.], 1958.

Rodríguez, Emilio A. "Games We Played in Ybor City." *La Gaceta*, June 27, 1997.

Rodríguez, Francisco. Quoted in *The Immigrant World of Ybor City*, by Gary R. Mormino and George E. Pozzetta. Urbana: University of Illinois Press, 1987.

Rodríguez, Gus. "The Sounds and Characters of Ybor City." *La Gaceta*, June 27, 1997.

Rodríguez, Wilfredo. Quoted in *Tampa Tribune*, May 22, 1981.

Sánchez, Al. Taped interview by Robert P. Ingalls, December 20, 2001. In possession of authors.

Sanfeliz, José Ramón. "Life History of José Ramón Sanfeliz." Typescript of interview (c. 1936) by Federal Writers' Project. Special Collections, University of South Florida Library.

Santos, Manuel. Quoted in *Tampa Tribune*, January 2, 1968.

Scaglione, Alex. Quoted in *The Immigrant World of Ybor City*, by Gary R. Mormino and George E. Pozzetta. Urbana: University of Illinois Press, 1987.

"Scolaro, Estefano" (a fictional character based on Alfonso Coniglio). Quoted in *The Truth about Them*, by Jose Yglesias. New York: World Publishers, 1971.

Stelzner, Hermann G., and Danio Bazo. "Oracle of the Tobacco Bench." *Southern Speech Journal* 31 (Winter 1965).

Tamargo, Manuel. Quoted in *Tampa Tribune*, September 15, 1977.

Tampa Cigar Manufacturers' Association. *Tampa Morning Tribune,* November 21, 1920.

———. *Tampa Morning Tribune,* November 27, December 7, 1931.

Tyrell, Reverend William J. Report to Bishop William Kenny, 1911, Records of the Catholic Church, Diocese of St. Augustine, P.K. Yonge Library, University of Florida, Gainesville.

U.S. Immigration Commission. *Immigrants in Industries—Part 14: Cigar and Tobacco Manufacturing.* Washington, D.C.: Government Printing Office, 1911.

Valdés, Armando, Jr., and Armando Valdés, Sr. Quoted in *Tampa Tribune Florida Accent*, December 14, 1969.

Valdés-Domínguez, Fermín. Entry (March 1897) in *Diario de soldado.* 5 vols. Havana: Universidad de La Habana, 1972–74.

Valdez, Virgilio. Quoted in *Tampa Times*, February 20, 1973.

Vega Díaz, José. Quoted in *Tampa Tribune*, May 14, 1979.

Winter, Nevin O. *Florida, the Land of Enchantment.* Boston: Page Company, 1918.

Women's Home Mission Society. *Eighteenth Annual Report.* Nashville, 1904.

Yglesias, Jose. *A Wake in Ybor City.* New York: Holt, Rinehart, and Winston, 1963.

———. Quoted in *Hard Times: An Oral History of the Great Depression*, by Studs Terkel. New York: Pantheon Books, 1970.

———. *The Truth about Them.* New York: World Publishers, 1971.

———. "A Latin Delight Survives in Tampa." *New York Times*, February 24, 1974.

———. "The Radical Latino Island in the Deep South." *Nuestro* 1 (August 1977).

———. "La Nochebuena: The Best of Nights." *Nuestro* 1 (December 1977).

———. Quoted in "He Misses Tampa as It Used to Be." *Tampa Magazine* (October 1981).

———. *One German Dead.* Leeds, Mass.: Eremite Press, 1988.

———. "A Trilogy Takes Its Playwright Home Again." *New York Times*, April 23, 1989.

———. "Buscando un sueño de Tampa a Nueva York." Translation by Ana Varela-Lago. *Más* 3 (July–August 1991).

———. "Martí in Ybor City." *José Martí in the United States: The Florida Experience*, edited by Louis A. Pérez. Tempe: Arizona State University Press, 1995.

Robert P. Ingalls is professor of history at the University of South Florida, Tampa. He is the author of *Urban Vigilantes in the New South: Tampa, 1881– 1936* (UPF, 1993).

Louis A. Pérez, Jr., is J. Carlyle Sitterson Professor of History at the University of North Carolina at Chapel Hill. He is the author of numerous books, including *On Becoming Cuban: Identity, Nationality, and Culture* (1999) and *Winds of Change: Hurricanes and the Transformation of Nineteenth-Century Cuba* (2001).